Praise for *Shifting Context*

"This book is very timely. Women must step forward—now more than ever. Women and men who dare must lead us out of the toxic patriarchy into a world where the divine feminine intelligence has as much room, potency, and validation as the healthy masculine. This is the Sophia Century, and this is one of the books that can lead us all there."

—Lynne Twist, Co-Founder, The Pachamama Alliance, Founder and President, Soul of Money

"*Shifting Context* extends the ideas that I offered in my books *Paradigm Found* and *From Outrage to Courage*. It describes many useful principles, such as leading in terms of values, listening, and embodying. It celebrates the sheroes and heroes leading grassroots movements around the world. As I learned as president of the Global Fund for Women, these are the people who can truly make positive localized change as they take on our most intractable issues."

—Anne Firth Murray, Founding President of the Global Fund for Women, and author

"*Shifting Context: Leadership Springs from Within* is an important book at an important time in history. Research consistently shows that countries who seriously invest in women's and girls' empowerment get a dramatic return on their investment financially, socially, and in all ways that matter for a civil society. The women featured in this book are exemplars of that important investment! It will inspire you, move you, and remind you of the hidden power that women have to make all of our lives better. Kudos to Linda and Barbara for their essential leadership in this movement for social entrepreneurship!"

—Rayona Sharpnack, Founder/CEO at Institute for Gender Partnership and Women's Leadership, Inc.

Shifting Context is a *gift* for every one of us committed to creating a better future. Inspiring and actionable lessons are drawn from the lived stories of people from all around the world— urging us to speak up, make tough choices, live into our leadership potential, and embrace the most important challenges of our times. I will hold these stories—and the courageous people in them—in my heart as a testament to how I can become a more conscious, loving, and daring leader myself."

—Steven Kowalski, PhD, Founder, Creative License Consulting Services; author, *Creative Together* (May 2022)

"This book could not be more important or timely. Linda and Barbara provide an explicit pathway for every reader— especially women—to find their voice and transform the way they live. Shifting context is everything. As a professor teaching leadership courses at Santa Clara University, I have witnessed firsthand the unstoppable power that comes with a shift in context. This book is filled with real stories that inspire and enable the change that is urgently needed in today's world. I highly recommend giving this book to every person you care about."

—Phyllis Brock, Principal, Highland Team Consulting and Adjunct Professor at Santa Clara University

"During years of observing, practicing, learning, and teaching the principles of leadership, Linda Alepin and Barbara Key noticed the ways their students absorbed and applied those principles to their own lives and life missions. Linda and Barbara were able to identify patterns of belief, which led to altered practices, which in turn became amazing results. Now they have created a path we can *all* follow to become world-changing leaders. Illustrating principles with stories that we can relate to, and generously providing questions that allow the reader to apply the lessons to their own lives, make this volume both inspirational and practical—what a gift to us all!"

—Linda Lubin Thompson, President, L2T Leadership Development

"Linda and Barbara are inspiring the readers to listen to their inner messages and step up and lead. They introduce the new generation of leaders, leaders for our time and current challenges. They astutely focus on the common characteristics of these leaders that reveal their core values, what they care about, how they embody their purpose and inspire others to follow."

—Dr. Mehrad Nazari, author of *Enlightened Negotiation*

"'Our promise is that there will be leadership inspiration and learning beyond any you have experienced,'" the authors write in the introduction to *Shifting Context*. I've known Linda Alepin for thirty years, and she delivers. If you want to lead change effectively, read this book!"

—Paola Gianturco, photojournalist and author

"*Shifting Context* is a celebration of the best, most effective, life-giving ways of leading: from the courage of the heart on behalf of the world. As Linda and Barbara show, the invisible sides of leadership get less attention, yet they are key to discovering what truly matters, to taking the next step even when confidence lags behind. In these inspiring stories, the women discover their innate wisdom, often buried or held back until they shift context, the mindsets that drive their behavior and results. These are stories of women who didn't believe but came to believe in themselves. Communicating with ethics and integrity, these leaders empowered others in trustworthy ways to take on issues, change the conversation, collaborate, dream new dreams, and produce results.

—Karen Wilhelm Buckley, Principal Organizational Development Consultant and host of the Wisdom and Power of Women Leaders

"Answering the simple question 'What do you truly care about?' is no easy task. Some leadership books provide exercises to coach us towards our answer; others seek to inspire us through the leadership journeys of others. *Shifting Context: Leadership Springs from Within* does both—combining the power of storytelling with a structure for personal reflection that pushes us to think differently, dream, and birth our own values-based leadership story."

—Jodi Morris, Success Coach & Founder, Connecting Growth Globally

Shifting CONTEXT

Leadership Springs from Within

LINDA T. ALEPIN & BARBARA E. KEY

Published by:

You as a Global Leader

TUCSON, ARIZONA

Copyright © 2022 Linda Alepin & Barbara Key

ISBNs: 979-8-9850805-0-6 (print)
979-8-9850805-1-3 (ebook)

Edited by Carol A. Rosenberg
Cover and interior by Gary A. Rosenberg
www.thebookcouple.com

Printed in the United States of America

In loving memory of Ron
I am who I am because of your love,
friendship, and caring.

—BEK

To Ronald, the love of my life,
father of my children, and best friend
Thank you for being the ever-present supporter
of my career and global efforts.

—LTA

In gratitude to the many women leaders around
the world who are featured in this book, we will
be contributing part of the book's proceeds to the
International Women Leaders for the World fund.

—LTA & BEK

Contents

Foreword

by Barry Zane Posner

FULL DISCLOSURE: I played a very small part in getting this research and book launched, and like so many extraordinary adventures, it began with saying, "Yes," and in that regard, this is an important "foreword" for Linda and Barbara's book—say "yes" and all things are possible. All the remarkable examples and stories in this book only happened because the people involved said "yes" to themselves as being both "worthy and enough," and to paraphrase Robert Frost, that made all the difference in their shifting context and having their leadership spring from within.

The people you will meet in this book are not well known or particularly famous, yet they share some remarkable characteristics with all the renowned leaders in history. Take a moment and name a historical leader whom you greatly admire. Who would that person be?

In our research we've asked thousands of people to do this. Although no single leader receives a majority of the nominations, in the United States, the two most frequently mentioned are Abraham Lincoln and Martin Luther King Jr.

Other historical leaders who've made the list include Aung San Suu Kyi, Susan B. Anthony, Benazir Bhutto, César Chávez, Winston Churchill, Mahatma Gandhi, Mikhail Gorbachev, Nelson Mandela, Golda Meir, His Holiness the Dalai Lama, J. Robert Oppenheimer, His Holiness Pope John Paul II, Eleanor Roosevelt, Franklin D. Roosevelt, Mother Teresa, Margaret Thatcher, and Archbishop Desmond Tutu.

What do leaders such as these have in common? Among these most admired leaders, one quality stands out above all else. The most striking similarity we've found—and surely, it's evident to you—is that the list is populated by people with *strong beliefs about matters of principle.* They all have, or had, unwavering commitment to a clear set of values. They all are, or were, passionate about their causes. The lesson from this simple exercise is unmistakable. The people who are admired most are the ones who believed strongly in something and were willing to stand up for their beliefs.*

Famous figures from history, of course, aren't the only leaders with strong beliefs on matters of principle. All the leaders in this book share this quality, no matter what status they may have achieved. These are stories of individuals who remained true to deeply held values. Becoming a leader means finding out what your core beliefs and values are. You have to understand what you deeply believe in. People won't follow you, or even pay much attention to you, if you don't have any strong beliefs. Often because of cultural norms, socioeconomic status or conditions, gender stereotyping, and institutional racism,

---

* James M. Kouzes and Barry Z. Posner. *The Leadership Challenge: How to Make Extraordinary Things Happen in Organizations* (Wiley, 2017).

it is difficult to always stand by one's principles. As we heard from one of the leaders we studied:

> *I ignored my heart and didn't listen to my own voice. I was a walking corpse. But I've come to understand that everyone has beliefs and values, and that in order for people to lead they've got to connect with them and be able to express them. This means that I have to let people know and understand what my thoughts are so that I can become a good leader. How can others follow me if I'm not willing to listen to my own inner self? Now, I let others know what I think is important and how hard I'm willing to fight for my values.*

Being a leader means speaking out on matters of values and conscience. But to speak out, you have to know what to speak about. To stand up for your beliefs, you have to know what you stand for. To walk the talk, you have to have a talk to walk. To do what you say, you have to know what you want to say. To earn and sustain personal credibility, you must first be able to clearly articulate deeply held beliefs.

You must know what you care about. If you don't care, how can you expect others to do so? If you don't burn with desire to be true to something you hold passionately, how can you expect commitment from others? And until you get close enough to the flame to feel the heat, how can you know the source? You can only be authentic when you lead according to the principles that matter most to you. Otherwise, you're just putting on an act.

Once, when my colleague and coauthor Jim Kouzes and I were discussing the origins of leadership, our conversation went something like this:

Jim: I think leadership begins with discontent.

Barry: That's too dismal a view for me. I think leadership begins with caring.

Jim: Okay, then, let's look up *caring* in the dictionary.

When we looked up the word *care*, we discovered that the first meaning of the word was "suffering of mind: GRIEF." There it was. Suffering and caring, discontent and concern, all come from one source. We realized that what we were both saying is that leadership begins with something that grabs hold of you and won't let go.*

As you read the stories and learn the lessons of experience from the leaders featured in this book, you will see that deep within them there was something that they held dear, were willing to fight for, to suffer and sacrifice for, to grieve if lost and to shout with joy when achieved. They had to explore their inner territory, and Linda and Barbara so poignantly and personally bring us along these leaders' journeys, exploring their inner territory, taking us into those places in their hearts and soul where they discovered their core truths.

On December 1, 1955, Rosa Parks sat still and, by doing so, set in motion a series of events that changed the course of history. By refusing to give up her seat on the Cleveland Avenue bus in Montgomery, Alabama, she precipitated a year-long protest and boycott, helped to elevate the young Martin Luther King, Jr. to prominence, and infused new energy into

---

* James M. Kouzes and Barry Z. Posner, *Everyday People. Extraordinary Leadership: How to Make a Difference Regardless of Your Title, Role, or Authority* (Wiley, 2021).

the Civil Rights movement. Reflecting on her actions and as evident in the actions of the leaders Linda and Barbara highlight in this book, three very important lessons about courage and leadership emerge.*

The first lesson is that *little acts can have huge impact.* Rosa Parks' actions weren't strategic or grand. They weren't self-promotional or manipulative. They weren't calculated or premeditated. Examine her actual behaviors—staying seated, saying "no," and willingly submitting to being arrested—and you can see that they are actions within everyone's grasp. They don't require big budgets, off-site strategic planning retreats, endless planning sessions, or huge armies. They require only a personal decision and the will to stick with it.

The second lesson is that *one person can make a difference.* By her refusal to move from her seat, Rosa Parks demonstrated the power of one person. She was not wealthy, a rebel-rouser, or a visible Civil Rights leader. She was a local activist, a good neighbor, a seamstress on her way home from work. *Shifting Context* is full of stirring stories of regular people just like Rosa Parks and encouragement for how we all have the potential to change the world—or at least a little piece of it.

The third lesson is that *courageous acts flow from beliefs.* Rosa Parks didn't get on the bus that day to get arrested, she got on the bus to go home, and the reason she didn't move was because her feet were tired; she was tired of being treated unfairly. Her refusal to move was an act of courage that emerged from within. She was committed to deeply rooted beliefs, to a set of guiding principles that were not only dear to

---

* James M. Kouzes and Barry Z. Posner, *A Leader's Legacy* (Wiley, 2006).

her, but also at the very core of a nation. Rosa Parks decided that day to test the truth of these fundamental ideals. So many of the stories in this book are examples of how people found that "something that they couldn't let go of" and their leadership was simply courage-in-action.

When someone or something challenges one of your deeply held beliefs and you grab hold of that opportunity right then and there to confront it, you have a Rosa Parks Moment. It doesn't have to be about something as monumental as freedom and justice, but it does have to be something that is extraordinarily important to you. It has to be a time when you say to yourself, "Enough is enough. I'm not going to take it anymore." And you have to be resolute about it. No fence sitting. No hemming and hawing. No equivocating. This is the moment; this is the time when you *have to* act.

As you read *Shifting Context* and learn about the remarkable lives and stories of people who are making a difference, ask yourself when was the last time you fought for a value that you cherished? When was the last time you were resolute in the face of stern resistance? And you also have to ask yourself, are you ready? Reading this book and taking seriously the appreciative inquiry questions asked at the end of each chapter will help prepare you for that moment.

It's the Rosa Parkses of the world who truly make the difference, and we are all capable of becoming leaders. The challenges that confront us in these troubled times aren't going to evaporate like the fog on a summer morning. They require a lot more of us if we're to overcome them. They demand that we make tough choices. They demand that we make sure we're clear about what we value and believe in. They demand that we take personal initiative when those values are challenged. They demand that we focus on the little things we do each day to be true to ourselves. They demand resilience and determination. Each and every one of us matters. Even the very simplest of actions can ripple through society creating waves of change.

—Barry Zane Posner
Accolti Professor of Leadership at the Leavey School of Business at Santa Clara University

Acknowledgments

We acknowledge all those who have contributed to the success of the transformational leadership education program Women Leaders for the World (WLW). Without exception, every minute, every effort, and every monetary contribution made to the program was essential to its success. We are grateful to the organization How Women Lead for their continuing operation of the program for women globally.

Barbara recognizes Bob Dunham, Andrea Bordenca, and others at the Institute for Generative Leadership for introducing her to practices that allowed the "real" leader within to emerge. She also recognizes the Strozzi Institute for showing her how to be centered in her life.

Linda acknowledges Barbara Fittipaldi for introducing her to transformational leadership education through her firm, Center for New Futures. The many years spent working with Barbara provided me with a sound foundation from which to cofound Global Women's Leadership Network.

Preface

Progress to remedy injustices is taking too long. It has been over half a century since Marvin Gaye released his consciousness-raising album, *What's Going On*. NPR has said that his song by the same title "helped change the national conversation."[1] Unfortunately, the themes Marvin Gaye explored in that album are just as relevant today—racial injustice, drug addiction, ecological damage, debilitating poverty, and, of course, unpopular wars. The world is still experiencing all those issues in addition to human rights violations and a global pandemic. At times, it feels like our planet is the *Titanic*, heading for a field of icebergs.

While Gaye sang about America's problems in 1971, today, with instantaneous communications, the scope is not confined to the borders of the United States. The Black Lives Matter movement has focused attention on unlawful police actions in the United States, while in Myanmar, the Rohingya people are dying and being savaged at the hands of the military. Some media are calling the Israeli-Palestinian conflict an example of ethnic cleansing as much as a fight over territorial rights.

Even while there has been an alarmingly rapid increase in opioid addiction in the United States, the United Nations reported that "Drug use increased more rapidly within developing countries over the 2000-2018 period, than in developed countries."[2] The same article cited "poverty, limited education and social marginalization," as increasing the risk of drug usage.

If that's not enough to alarm you, the gap between rich and poor is widening in the world and in the United States. In economic terms, as of the early twenty-first century, the North—with one-quarter of the world population—controls four-fifths of the income earned anywhere in the world.[3] Moreover, in its article "9 World Poverty Statistics That Everyone Should Know," LifeWater says that, "Ten percent of the world's population live on less than $2 per day."[4] The 2011 U.S. Occupy Movement was about "social and economic inequality, greed, corruption and the undue influence of corporations on government—particularly from the financial services sector," according to Leslie E. Sekerka in *Ethics Is a Daily Deal.*[5]

What's more, human rights violations abound. According to C. Bradbury-Jones and L. Isham, the lockdown imposed to deal with COVID-19 has granted greater freedom to abusers.[6] Several media reports indicate a surge in cases of domestic violence in various countries. According to J. Kagi, though a drop was observed in the overall crime rates in Australia, the domestic abuse rates increased by 5 percent.[7] Different states in the United States also reported an increase of about 21 to 35 percent in domestic violence.[8]

While all of this is occurring, indigenous peoples like the Inuit of Canada and the Achuar from the Amazon are losing their territory, their culture, their language, and even their means of livelihood to the encroachment of civilization and the search for natural resources on native lands. And the effects of climate change are evident around the globe. Disasters are getting stronger and more frequent. Droughts are lasting longer. Weather patterns are less predictable. Farming practices that were once stable are no longer effective. Smaller harvests leave families with less to eat and sell.[9]

What can be done about these and other issues?

The world's problems are calling for new ways of leading that take what people care about from being just personal ideals to being reality. The world needs role models who have taken on issues and produced results. Best practices from leaders around the globe need to be publicized and available. Social change happens at the fringes of society as well as through the efforts of large institutions such as the Bill & Melinda Gates Foundation. It happens in the smaller nongovernmental organizations (NGOs) led by passionate people working at the grassroots level. In this book, we felt it was important to share examples of leaders that most people can identify with, rather than "bigger than life" leaders such as Bill Gates. We are not motivated to act toward goals that look impossible. Rather, when we learn how ordinary people with fewer resources can have social impact, action is more likely.

Shifting Context illustrates real social change and the leadership principles that contribute to it. If you are passionate about creating social impact, *Shifting Context: Leadership Springs from Within* is for you. The stories of leaders from around the world bring social change efforts to life. They bear witness to people who have taken on the challenge of demonstrating that leadership starts from within.

These courageous people have adopted new ways of listening, of shedding limiting beliefs, and of connecting deeply with what they care about. They are examples of people living up to one's leadership potential and, through that process, creating extraordinary results. The book makes the invisible visible—it looks behind the actions of leaders to expose the leadership approaches that made them successful. It is our hope that this book cultivates a belief in you that *you* can overcome even seemingly insurmountable problems and effect change.

Storytelling, the main approach in this book, is recognized as a powerful way to create social impact. A Georgetown University course called Social Impact Storytelling states that:

> History has shown that stories are inextricably linked to what it means to be human. Before there was formal communication, there were stories. It should come as no surprise, then, that social movements and organizations like nonprofits, foundations, and socially responsible businesses are now working to leverage stories as a strategic tool to advance important missions. Effective stories are powerful because they drive action: spurring donations, mobilizing supporters, and more. By building emotional connections, stories bring to life the work of the issues we care so much about in ways that other forms of communication cannot.[10]

We embarked on the writing of the book as the logical next stage of our self-expression and a way to provide our leadership wisdom. It takes us each closer to what our hearts yearn for. "Care abouts" are the most important values in our lives. They drive us to stand for that value and to initiate action toward fulfilling it.

What are our "care abouts"?

Well, Barbara's deepest care is for the freedom to be able to express herself and lead others to find their own voices. She wants to be authentically herself and have others feel that they can be true to themselves. She desires a world where every person can experience freedom.

As for Linda, she feels a deep care for justice in the world. This caring began when, as a woman in business, she witnessed and experienced discrimination. The scope of injustice, however, became more evident when she began working with people from around the world. Linda wants to see a world of peace, love, and justice for everyone.

I (Linda) founded a nonprofit called Global Women's Leadership Network to train women around the world to lead. Barbara joined me a couple of years later, and we worked for that nonprofit for more than a decade. Though we parted from that organization several years ago to design a new training curriculum that could be both virtual and in person, the nonprofit continues the transformational leadership mission. We still support the international graduates of the program through a donor advised fund called the International Women Leaders for the World fund. A portion of the proceeds from this book will be donated to support that effort.

We came to see this book as a means to share the stories of the program participants so that they could serve as role models to motivate others to step into their leadership. Friends gave us advice. For example, John Montgomery, a benefits governance lawyer as well as an author, said, "You do not write the book; the book writes you." Over the course of our book-writing journey, we learned the truth of this statement. We had to see deeper into others and into ourselves.

We started writing about the secret strengths people exhibited—what they did and the qualities they had. Somewhere along the way, we entered a dark period, a period of hopelessness in which we doubted that anything we wrote would be "good enough" or even make a difference. Finally, we emerged into a time when we focused the stories on who people were being—and who *we* were being. Overall, our writing journey reminds us of a passage from *Encouraging the Heart* by Barry Posner and Jim Kouzes, which compares becoming a leader to becoming a painter:

> When first learning to lead, we paint what we see outside of ourselves, the exterior landscape. We read biographies and autobiographies about famous leaders. We read trade books by experienced executives and dedicated scholars . . .
>
> We do all this to master the fundamentals, the tools, and the techniques. We're clumsy at first, failing more than succeeding . . .
>
> Then it happens. Somewhere along the way . . . We awaken to the frightening thought that the words are not ours, that the vocabulary is someone else's, that the technique is right out of the text but not straight from the heart.
>
> This is a terrifying moment. Having invested so much time and energy in learning to do all the right things, we suddenly see that they're no longer serving us well . . . We stare into the darkness of our inner landscape, and we begin to wonder what lies inside.

For aspiring leaders, this awakening initiates a period of intense exploration... And if you surrender to it, after exhausting experimentation and often painful suffering you come to the third period. From all those abstract strokes on the canvas emerges an expression of self that is truly your own.[11]

The second period that Posner and Kouzes describe—the time of introspection—was the hardest for us in writing this book. We were not yet in a mood of ambition. We were bordering on resignation that our book would never be. We stumbled along doing interviews and composing chapters. Fortunately, we granted each other grace when we had a misstep. We gave each other unmerited love and unconditional acceptance.

Then came a turning point: During our interview with Mehrad Nazari, author of *Enlightened Negotiation,* he described his own journey of writing a book that gave our work a renewed spark of life.

Soon, our friend Karen Wilhelm Buckley, Principal Organizational Development Consultant and host of the Wisdom and Power of Women Leaders, suggested using quotes from the interviews to title our chapters. Sometimes all it takes is a small dose of inspiration. What can inspiration blossom into if one fertilizes it with wonderment, effort, and caring? It helped us to see that we were "enough." Enough to write the book. Enough to overcome fear. Enough to let inspiration saturate our beings. Enough to shine a light on the humanity of leadership. Enough to feel and embody what we were writing. Enough to believe that what we have to say was important to the world!

We have dedicated much of our lives to serving all types of leaders around the world. It has been through our consulting to businesses, facilitating workshops, holding coaching sessions, and completing joint projects that we have honed our understanding of what it is to be a leader for the twenty-first century. We have spent decades studying, teaching about, and practicing leadership. Our greatest joy is when our students share their accomplishments achieved by applying new ways of leading. The book became an expression of our love for the courageous women and like-minded men we have had the honor to know.

INTRODUCTION

Standing in a Stream

WHY DOES A PETITE MAASAI WOMAN from a remote village want to attend a program called Women Leaders for the World (WLW) in the United States? Does she see her work rescuing young women from female genital mutilation (FGM) having influence far beyond her local environs? Is it her heart and her courage that lead her to choose a path to that class? Does it involve the hand of a divine spirit?

How does a course that attracts those with heart and courage come to be? In the mid-1990s, I (Linda), a tired Silicon Valley executive, was on my way home. I was CEO of an early Internet startup, and it had been one of those roller-coaster days that occur so often in the world of entrepreneurs. I knew that my kids and husband waited at home and that my currently frayed state of mind was not conducive to being a loving mother and wife. So, I stopped in a park off the freeway where I had pushed baby carriages in my younger days.

I knew there was a way to get down to a stream under a grove of trees. Once there, I found a sandbar where I could stand, close my eyes, and become quiet. My attention was drawn to the babbling of the brook, the leaves rustling in the trees, the songs of birds, and the feel of the breeze on my face. As I relaxed into nature's arms, an image of women from all over the world dressed in native garb and walking in a beautiful rose garden entered my mind. They were talking about studying leadership together, and they would be able to support each other, even when apart, through emerging technologies.

I went home that night to tell my husband about the image and what it might be about. The next day and for several years afterward, I talked about my vision of global women leaders. I played out my life. The startup collapsed. I joined a nascent leadership consulting company. I began learning about the issues of poverty, violence against women, and more that plague the world. I became an adjunct professor at a Jesuit university—Santa Clara University (SCU). The mission was to create leaders of competence, conscience, and compassion.

In 2004, with help from a mentor at SCU, Dean Dr. Barry Posner, the picture from that day in the stream became a reality. The Global Women's Leadership Network (GWLN) was born. Women Leaders for the World (WLW) was the main program. Helen Nkuraiya, the Maasai woman mentioned earlier, was part of the seventh class in 2011.

More than ten years later in a seminar with Joseph Jaworski, author of the book *Synchronicity*, I told this story of the stream and the vision. Upon hearing about it, he said, "This is one of the best stories about the influence of 'source' that I have ever heard." By *source*, I know from studying with Joseph that he means spirit—that connection to one's higher self or to a spiritual being one believes in.

The people featured in this book are our personal friends and clients. They represent many walks of life, cultures, races, industries, and countries. While this book is written from the perspective of North American Caucasian women, we have attempted to represent a "whole world" perspective. We hold a joint belief that it will be the local leaders who can solve a vast spectrum of local problems and, in addition, provide profound wisdom to our planet.

Leaders' journeys often follow similar paths. Despite wanting to accomplish a vision, people start off doubting themselves. William Miller, author and expert in human-centered innovation, spoke these words in a seminar attended by Linda: "Not enough is the mega pandemic of the world." Every leader featured in this book finally reached a point of knowing they were "enough." Their connection to what they cared deeply about drew them forward. As you will learn in this book, it is possible to discover what we care deeply about and align our actions with those cares.

How This Book Is Structured

Activists are people who work to bring about social change. They are those who care deeply about a particular issue. They want to make a difference in the community, country, or the world. This book reveals new ways to get results—by starting with yourself as a leader.

Yes, there are stories of how others made progress on social issues. That in aßnd of itself is important to fuel social change. There are many other ways. Context shifts are some of the most powerful. Even small shifts in context can create major change in results. Context shifts are more about who one is "being" than what one is "doing." Building on what one cares about through context shifts can cause breakthroughs and greater social impact.

Following Chapter 1, which discusses shifting context, the book is divided into six parts, each of which corresponds to the type of context shift the stories illustrate. Thus, there are parts devoted to discovering what one cares about, developing one's vision, enhancing listening, generating resilience, and so on.

Most of the stories in this book begin when the story's subject attended a transformational leadership course. This started their journey of becoming a leader who dares to take on bigger and more challenging social issues. This book is a means for you to adopt the principles that our sheroes and heroes learned in their course. As you read the stories, we encourage you to see yourself as a leader in each of the stories. How does the shift in context illustrated in each story apply to your leadership and your life? How can you strengthen your leadership by applying the essence of the context shift for yourself? The stories are sometimes preceded by or lead to relevant discussions to help make the leadership skills illustrated in the stories more actionable for you. Useful information on the issues and the countries of the stories is included as further background.

When we interviewed each person, the focus was on finding the best of their work as opposed to coming from what was wrong or broken. This is the foundation of the Appreciative Inquiry model. See "What Is Appreciative Inquiry (AI)?" on the following page. It steers away from locating a problem or what is not working and then attempting to fix it. Appreciative Inquiry is a well-researched transformational change model that originated in Case Western University in Ohio by David Cooperrider. This is the design model for all our work, ranging from writing this book to developing curriculum and facilitating workshops.

At the end of each chapter, you will find several Appreciative Inquiry questions for reflection. These are designed to stimulate thinking about and taking actions in concert with the leadership principles illustrated by the stories. They call for discovering the best from the past, dreaming about the future, designing how to make that dream happen, and delivering through continuing to be open to change. Reflection leads to actions, which create results.

What Is Appreciative Inquiry (AI)?

Why is Appreciative Inquiry a valuable tool to prompt reflection? According to *The Appreciative Inquiry Handbook:*

> "Appreciative Inquiry is the co-evolutionary, co-operative search for the best in people, their organizations, and the relevant world around them . . . AI involves the art and practice of asking questions that strengthen a system's capacity to apprehend, anticipate and heighten positive potential . . . AI practice focuses on the speed of the imagination and innovation. Instead of negative, critical, and spiraling diagnoses commonly used in our organizations . . . there is discovery, dream, design and deliver."[12]

An Appreciative Inquiry typically goes through the following four stages:

1. **Discover:** Appreciating and valuing the best of "what is." Information and stories are gathered about what is working well.

2. **Dream:** Envisioning what might be. How do we want things to be for the future?

3. **Design:** Determining what should be. How can we move from where we are now to this vision of the future that we have created? How can we put the ideas into practice? Who will be involved?

4. **Deliver (or Destiny):** Innovating what will be. In this phase, practical strategies or projects are put into practice and space is created for ideas to flow and develop. There is an emphasis on empowering and encouraging people to act and carry forward their own ideas.[13]

We believe that it is more important than ever for people who are leaders in their own life, in business, in academia, in civil society, and in families to have role models who demonstrate fundamentally new ways of thinking and acting. It is time for all of us to question the twentieth-century leadership characteristics of being solely focused on growing business, making money, beating competition, and—at all times—maintaining control. It is time, in fact, to listen to voices from all over the world, not just North America. It is time for leaders to let hearts and intuition be fully expressed. It is time for women leaders and like-minded men to be valued for their unique characteristics.

"Your generation of leaders will know that everyone on this earth is born with the potential to lead. And that is a deep and fundamental shift, a shift worth celebrating. Every man and every woman on this earth is born to lead. A leader's greatest obligation is to make possible an environment where people's minds and hearts can be inventive, brave, human and strong, where people can aspire to do useful and significant things, where people can aspire to change the world."

—CARLY FIORINA, CEO OF HEWLETT PACKARD, JUNE 2, 2000 (Massachusetts Institute of Technology Commencement Address)

To lead during our challenging times requires each of us to become a leader who dares. Join us on that journey through this book. Our promise is that there will be leadership inspiration and learning beyond any you have experienced.

CHAPTER 1

Whole Woman, Whole Leader, Whole World

INVISIBLE FORCES ARE ACTING ON OUR LIVES. These forces shape actions, feelings, and thoughts. They determine how we interpret what is happening around us and how we react to them. These forces are contexts. They are a set of beliefs, many of which we are unaware of that dictate how we think, what we pay attention to, and consequently how we behave. Learning to shift the given context of a situation is the key to leading, particularly in turbulent times.

How does context work? Imagine you are sitting in a college geology class and the professor mentions the word *depression*. An image of the Grand Canyon might come to mind. In the next hour, moving to a psychology class, the same word conjures up a distressing mental condition. Or, later that day, sitting in an economics class, it suggests the early twentieth-century collapse of the world's financial system.

This single, relatively simple word has several meanings. Is it any wonder that when several people are affected by a set of circumstances, each can have a vastly different interpretation? Is it any wonder that they may take vastly different actions?

Our "life's context" built up from years of experiences and knowledge colors and frames our perceptions. It determines what aspects of a situation the brain even registers. There have been many experiments that illustrate how our "frame of reference" affects our perceptions.

Many people have seen images that can be viewed in two different ways. Perhaps the most well-known of these is the image called "My Wife and My Mother-in-law."* Some people see a young woman while others see a "hag." In 2015, there was "the dress" that made rounds on social media. Some people saw it as black and blue while others saw it as gold and white. Research eventually established that the differences were based on what assumptions a person's mind made about the lighting conditions.[14] Our mind tricks us into believing something about the picture that is not true. A more intricate example is the "Monkey Business Illusion," a video on YouTube and other online platforms; the viewer is asked to count how many times the players wearing white pass the ball. Take a moment to watch this video and listen to the commentary at the end. You may be surprised at what you focus on—or don't!**

---

* Yasemin Saplakoglu, "What You See in This Famous Optical Illusion Could Reveal How Old You Are," *LiveScience*, September 21, 2018, https://www.livescience.com/63645-optical-illusion-young-old-woman.html.

** "The Monkey Business Illusion," Daniel Simons, April 28, 2021, video, 1:41, https://www.youtube.com/watch?v=IGQmdoK_ZfY.

Context Determines Action

Does our accumulated life experience have more influence on our lives than just what we observe? Are experiences in early childhood determinants of future behavior? Does context from all parts of our life, in fact, determine, to a lesser or greater degree, our actions? Is it possible for us to build an alternate context and change our lives?

In childhood, I (Linda) was a bright young girl who received praise from my parents mostly when I had done something "perfectly." I came home from kindergarten with straight As, and my father said, "Wonderful! Go do it again!" A rhyme recited around my house was "Good, better, best, never take a rest until your good is better and your better best." My mother taught me how to iron sheets, fold hospital corners on the beds, and hang all the socks together on the clothesline. With this proximate context, was I destined for a type-A personality? Would I be ambitious and seeking to achieve success in business? Would I look for the smallest flaws in the work of others? How would I react when I was on a failing team?

I was once in a leadership class where we identified all the gender paradigms about women. There were many! Here are just a few:

✦ Women are not good at math.

✦ Women will get pregnant and leave their jobs.

✦ Women will need to go home early from work for childcare.

✦ Women are weak.

✦ Women are not good at sports.

We also identified some of our limiting thoughts about ourselves, such as:

✦ I am an impostor.

✦ I am not pretty.

✦ I have to be perfect.

After we covered the walls with flipchart paper, we had to pick the limiting thought that had the strongest grip on us. I chose "being perfect." Then we had to compose a three-minute skit that poked fun at this belief. I still remember my skit and how much relief I felt as I laughed at myself. Of course, the leadership class did not leave us there. We spent another two days imagining our world when we were free of this belief. We crafted big visions that would draw us forward. All the activities were designed to help us shift our life's context.

Another example of changing context is provided by Maame Afon Yelbert-Sai, who was born in Ghana. After completing high school in Ghana, she came to the United States to study at a college in Iowa. Imagine the context shifts she experienced.

Maame stayed in the United States and earned a master's degree from the Middlebury Institute of International Studies, Monterey (MIIS). She married, started a family, and went on to work for Global Fund for Women. Like so many young women, she was juggling her roles as mother, wife, and professional. She lived in a "siloed" way. Each role had its own context and its own "right" way to be.

As a junior member of staff, she felt a sense of powerlessness and as if she did not have a voice. Further, she did not believe her gifts were being fully utilized. These are typical feelings of people in organizations. The context is that you are "lesser than" because of your age, experience, title, gender, race, or other factors.

Maame was invited to participate in the transformational leadership education program Women Leaders for the World (WLW). She was introduced to the concept of Whole Woman, Whole Leader, Whole World. It lit a fire in her that she had not experienced before. She would build a movement around this concept. It would start with her. She would bring all of who she is to every experience, to all and everything she is becoming. Here was a holistic means of acknowledging fears, trials, successes, gifts, and talents. People could *be* whole and *see* the whole of who she was.

This was a new context for her life. She could proudly blend her African heritage with her American environment. In the leadership programs she coordinated and facilitated, she gave herself permission to use African concepts of leadership. One example is the Zulu greeting, Sawubona–Yebo Sawubona, which refer to "seeing each other" and acknowledging the fullness of who we are and where we come from. When you meet someone, you say, "*Sawubona*" (it is good to "see" you). In return they say, "*Yebo Sawubona*" (it is good to be seen). In essence this greeting is an intentional way of asking, "How are you really?"

Maame Afon felt comfortable remembering her roots and stepping out to be bold in new, challenging situations. She learned to see the gold in herself and others. She remembered her mother, who could always see the best in others, who called out the gold in them even when circumstances proved contrary. Maame shares the story of how her mother helped a neighbor go from nothing to later become a successful businessman. Maame dedicated herself to seeing the potential in people and in herself.

Today, Maame has her own consulting company: Management for Impact Leadership and Transformation (MILT). She has let her voice soar as a recording artist. She has been a model mother to her three children and has risen to the challenge of raising twins.

Ways to Shift Context

There are many ways to shift context, including caring about something, developing a vision, making a commitment, listening, and questioning, embodying leadership, and empowering interpretations (see Figure 1.1 on the following page). Varying aspects of these approaches will be discussed in later chapters. Let's take a brief look at each with some examples.

Identifying What You Care About (Your "Cares")

Finding out what you care about is fundamental to the process of shifting context. It is the anchor for employing all other approaches. So, how can you find out what you care deeply about?

There is an ancient Mayan and Middle Eastern tradition that purports to connect the heart and the brain. It starts by placing the palm of the hand over the heart and slowing

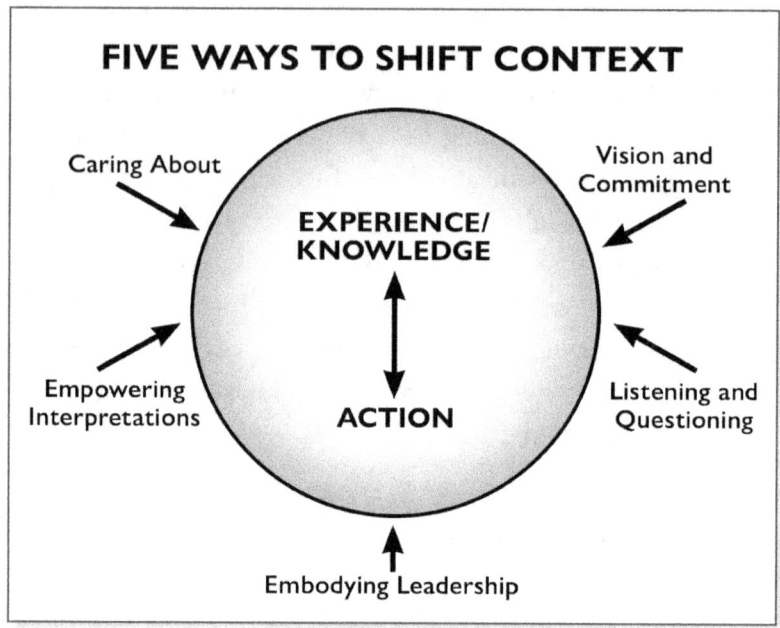

Figure 1.1. Five Ways to Shift Context and the Interrelationship Between Actions and Experience/Knowledge

the breath. According to author Gregg Branden, the theory behind this is that "awareness will always go to the place in the body where one feels the touch."[15] This exercise can be done alone or with a partner. Either silently or by having your partner speak, ask the question, "What do I care about?" or "What do you care about?" (The partner is a silent witness to the answer.) If you allow silence for a few seconds, the connection with what you care about may grow stronger. Listen to what comes up for you in this silence. Once you have identified something you care about, continue the exercise by asking the question two or three more times, looking for other cares.

For a different approach to identifying cares, you can look at younger years when you had more freedom to participate in your favorite pastimes. Divide a sheet of paper into three columns, labeling them as follows: column 1—early childhood to age six; column 2—ages 7 to 12; and column 3—ages 13 to 18. Under each column, write at least ten things you considered special activities at those ages. It may take a few days to complete these lists as you may not remember everything all at once.

Once you have a long list in each column, look for patterns. If you were always playing dolls in the early years, switched to pretending to be a doctor when you were a little older, and then volunteered at an animal shelter as a teen, your care may be nurturing. If you loved to dig in the sandbox, switched to hiking with your parents, and then became a kids' camp counselor, the care may be nature.

Another way to expose more about cares is to notice reactions to news events. Was your anger over the murder of George Floyd a reflection of a care for social justice? Was excitement at the announcement of a new smartphone a hint that technology advancement is important? Did Etna's latest eruption make you so curious that you could not wait to do in-depth research, an indication of a passion for geology?

Some people know what they care about at a young age. Others take years to discover what they care about. What is most important is using that care to initiate actions and to set a direction for life. You may have noticed that what one cares about is similar to one's core values. It becomes a true care when there is a commitment to follow the value with specific actions.

When we have a deep sense of caring about something, our actions can emanate from that care. The effect on actions of what a mother or father "cares about" is never more visible than when one of their children is in danger. Connection to those things people care about—in an emergency or in everyday life—has its effect on the type of action taken.

Knowing what you care about personally can be expanded into conversations about that topic. Conversations about care can create meaningful relationships based on mutual understanding. If you are leading a movement, knowing that a fellow activist cares deeply about social justice may help you engage them in a particular activity. If another values fairness because a family member was mistreated by the police, you can see if writing a new article on fairness resonates with them. If an employee cares about their father-daughter relationship and takes an annual fishing trip with her dad, her manager, aware of that care, can ensure that her vacation is scheduled when the season opens. Having a deeper understanding of what others care about and relating to others through those cares creates trust and better collaboration.

Your Vision and Making a Commitment

When you identify what you care about, it can be developed into a vision and a commitment. Vision and commitment are interrelated. According to *Merriam-Webster's Dictionary*, one definition of the word *vision* is "the act or power of imagination." Its definition of *commitment* is "an agreement or pledge to do something in the future." So, a vision often leads to a commitment.

A vision can be imagined about a nation, a community, a movement, a project, or a person. Famous visionary statements such as Mahatma Gandhi's "A free India" have had an impact on the course of history, altering millions of lives. Gandhi's words changed the context in which people lived. The early women's suffrage movement had a vision that included "equal access to education and employment, equality within marriage, and a married woman's right to her own property and wages, custody over her children and control over her own body."[16] So the right to vote was only a part of a much broader agenda.

John F. Kennedy's vision was a request for a *commitment*. He stood before Congress in May 1961 and said the United States "should commit itself to achieve the goal, before this decade is out, of landing a man on the Moon and returning him safely to the Earth."[17] This rallying cry mobilized a nation.

"Whole woman, whole leader, whole world" is a vision. It was adopted by Global Women's Leadership Network after cofounder Bonita Banducci envisioned this while swimming laps. Many times, ideas come to people while doing repetitive movements or when they get "quiet" such as in meditation. "Whole woman, whole leader, whole world" is a mantra that has become meaningful to those who attend the Women Leaders for the World (WLW) program. It has led to actions by several of the participants to integrate their life's roles.

Real commitment is a bridge. It transforms the mental picture or words about a vision into a series of actions. It can start with the simple act of talking to someone about the vision and possible ways it can happen. Making a commitment may make one aware that current actions are not taking one on a path toward the vision. The commitment creates a new mental framework and vantage point.

Listening and Questioning

Listening and asking questions are the fundamentals of communication. They are also two of the most powerful tools that leaders have to shift the culture and effectiveness of their organizations, communities, and movements.

Listening refers to what we hear as well as how it is registered. What is registered is highly filtered—mostly by being sifted against our past. Our listening is on automatic. We are normally not even aware of the automaticity. We are listening for agreement with what we already know. We tend to be judgmental about what we hear. There is so much going on in our heads that it is almost a miracle when what another person is saying actually gets through without being modified by all our filtering.

We can learn to listen in a different way. Once we are aware of the filtering process, we can begin to shape our listening. We can listen for opportunities—to apply our expertise, to add value, and to connect to other people. We can ask the speaker for further details in order to understand completely. We can tell the person what resonates with us about what they are saying. We can pause before responding to give our minds time to truly hear what was said.

Similarly, the questions we ask can be formed to create a more collaborative environment. When something goes wrong, we can easily fall into the trap of asking questions that can be interpreted as trying to place blame. Inadvertently, we may be causing people to become defensive. Or our questions can be loaded with assumptions with the result that the listener feels as if they are being led to some conclusion. Getting to the facts of a situation and avoiding the emotions of the moment takes expertise in forming questions.

We can ask questions to better understand another's point of view. We can ask open-ended questions that explore possibilities to expand thinking. We can ask different questions if we want incremental improvements versus radical new directions.

Leaders can become experts in tuning their listening and asking questions so that cultures of creativity and openness are fostered around them.

Making Empowering Interpretations

It is human nature to instantaneously attach an interpretation to everything we see, hear, and experience. Unfortunately, many of those interpretations are negative conclusions based on our filters. A conscious leader takes a second look at these automatic conclusions to see if there is a way to interpret the circumstances that forwards what they care about. An empowering interpretation is one that opens possibilities for positive action.

For example, what if the results of a survey about people's attitude toward solar energy shows that 60 percent of those surveyed do not want to install solar cells on their roofs? It would be easy to be discouraged by the high percentage and voice that viewpoint to people in your climate change group. Or, as a leader in the group, you could suggest that you recruit the 40 percent to be champions for solar installations.

Thoughtful leaders are also careful not to quickly add weight to negative rumors that circulate in organizations. This is not to say that they ignore facts, but rather that they stick to the facts and know that there are numerous ways to interpret them. There might be a rumor that a local lumber company has applied for a permit to cut down a grove of heritage trees. Instead of just trying to stop the rumor, a leader might call up both the company and the town hall to check if the rumor is true.

Embodying Leadership

Professional athletes are excellent examples of people who embody what they care about. Take, for instance, Rafael "Rafa" Nadal Parera, a Spanish professional tennis player. He started playing tennis at the age of three.[18] As an athletic youth, he also played soccer. Over time, with his uncle Toni's coaching, he gained phenomenal physical skills and mastery of tennis, which deepened his feelings for the sport. His commitment to the game grew, and he abandoned soccer. He began winning tournaments and turned professional at age fifteen. Today, watching Nadal, he is beauty in motion on the court. One sees that he lives for the game and the game lives within him. His thoughts, emotions, and physiology are in harmony. In fact, *embodiment* refers to "our interconnected system of thoughts, emotions, and neuromuscular physiology."[19]

Mehrad Nazari, author of *Enlightened Negotiation*, described embodiment to us as "the mind-heart connection." He says that it is a highly dynamic state that portrays our values. Embodiment is when your actions consistently reflect your values and your commitment, especially under pressure. In other words, your values animate being and all your actions. So, we might embody truth or a welcoming spirit if those are deep-seated values. Embodying leadership is about learning to lead from your authentic self. It involves working through the body to deeper levels of self-awareness and developing the capacity to be the leader you want to be and are committed to achieve. It is about a feeling of being whole.[20]

Embodying what we care about and leading from that interconnection does not occur overnight. There are three levels: awareness, cultivation, and integration. Like many aspects of leadership, it is a journey of self-discovery. At first, we identify what we care about. We may articulate it as "I care about family" or "I care about women being treated fairly." Over time, as we dig deeper, it may become "I care about loving relationships" or "I care about social justice." And, finally, in an insightful moment, it may morph into "I care about loving others and being loved" or "I care about women, including myself, being able to contribute to the world." The latter forms are more personal and more fully integrate the self.

How can we enhance our ability to embody what is important to us? There are various ways to prepare to embody what we care about. These include meditation, yoga, music, and somatic practices like centering. These bring a sense of peace that allows the mind and the body to connect. After many years of using these methods to bring that sense of peace, it becomes easier in stressful moments to create that state of mind and body connection.

Why is embodying what you care about an important part of leadership? Embodying your cares leads to congruency. It leads to actions that feel right in your mind and your body. It leads to one being more authentic and being seen as acting with integrity. Ultimately, embodying leadership leads to being able to act with others of like cares to produce extraordinary results.

APPRECIATIVE INQUIRY QUESTIONS TO PONDER

▦ *Discover*

✓ Using one of the methods on pages 14 and 15, discover two or three cares—things that give your life meaning.

▦ *Dream*

✓ What does the world look like when your vision for what you care about is fulfilled? Draw a vivid picture of what life is like when that is true.

▦ *Design*

✓ Make a list of actions that would lead to your vision and care being fulfilled, especially those that you could personally initiate.

▦ *Deliver*

✓ Commit to at least one activity in the next month that provides an opportunity to be involved in something you care about.

PART ONE

Care About

CHAPTER 2

I Am Who I Am

IN AUGUST 2000, MY LIFELONG PARTNER Ron Clausing and I (Barbara) attended a one-day workshop sponsored by the Institute for Generative Leadership (IGL)* led by Bob Dunham, its founder. It was our introduction to generative leadership. I heard one of the instructors say, "A generative leader is someone who engages in, and faithfully practices, a style of leadership that is observable, actionable, recurrent, and oriented to results that create value for the customer." This workshop introduced us to a new way of being as leaders in our respective careers and as lifelong partners.

At the end of the day, we are left feeling exhausted and asking ourselves, "Do we want to dedicate ourselves to becoming generative leaders?" After a few days of thought, we decided to embark on the journey of learning with the IGL community. It changed our lives and our relationship.

I Am Because of . . .

One of the first exercises I remember in IGL was declaring what I cared about. Ron and I did the exercise together. We

---

* For more information, visit https://generateleadership.com/.

cared about developing our relationship and having time for being together, for maintaining our health, and for fun and vacations. Once Ron and I had declared our cares, we engaged in the practice of saying them aloud to each other in a sincere tone. Doing so transferred our cares into commitments or promises, which we upheld until Ron's death.

In addition to our times at IGL, Ron and I attended Strozzi Institute.* There we further developed our commitments. I declared that I would practice stating my commitment at least once a day to embody it in my being. From then on, Ron and I maintained a daily practice of standing in front of a tree and individually stating our commitment. We chose a tree because it, like our commitments, was alive. We used the format we had been taught at Strozzi. My statement was, "I am a commitment to change with dignity." Our daily recitals reinforced our commitment. We held each other accountable to follow our words.

In my consulting business, I cared about guiding leaders of organizations to achieve results that would create the change they valued. For example, in one organization, the CEO declared that he would merge the operational functions of two not-for-profit organizations to reduce costs by 50 percent. While he declared this lofty goal every time he spoke to a group, he never followed through on what he said. Despite the numerous discussions we had about how important honesty was for a leader, he never changed his behavior. Eventually, he was fired. I could not understand what made it so difficult for leaders, like him, to take action to achieve the change they

---

* For more information, visit https://strozziinstitute.com/.

supposedly desired. What was missing? Today, I believe it was a commitment from the depth of his being, one from which to take observable, believable actions based on that deep commitment.

I had been a student of leadership courses, but nowhere had I learned the fundamental principle of being a generative leader—one who starts with and fulfills a commitment based on the cares housed in their heart. However, in time, Ron and I realized that holding a commitment in our heart was still insufficient to take new actions. This also held true for the leaders with whom I was consulting. During our week at Strozzi Institute, Ron and I learned about letting go of beliefs that were holding us back from new actions and results.

One evening, all the participants sat outside around a fire-pit and enacted "letting go." We wrote our limiting beliefs on strips of paper, tossed them into the fire, and silently watched as they disappeared in the flames. The act of throwing my piece of paper into the roaring fire was significant to me because I felt that those beliefs had been a major part of my identity. Past social conditioning has the strength of superglue!

My coauthor, Linda, and I have been studying the work of author Michael Singer, especially his book *The Untethered Soul Guided Journal: Practices to Journey Beyond Yourself.* "Letting go" requires all leaders to choose to free ourselves from the incessant chatter in our heads—for example, "I might fail if . . ." or any one of the old paradigms we heard throughout our personal and professional lives. Singer refers to this voice as "our roommate." The best way to free ourselves and to let go is to step back and notice the incessant chatter objectively. No matter what the voice is saying, it does not matter. It is still just a voice talking in your head. When I realize my voice from the past is just that—the past—I am free to move forward, accepting that "I am enough!"

Oh, that elusive feeling of being enough. I have been haunted by thoughts that I am not worthy, I do not measure up to other leaders, and I was not a good enough partner to Ron. Perhaps you can relate to such thoughts. Bob Dunham has been steadfast in his work with me to help free myself from these haunting thoughts and to be the leader I can become. My learning edge is, "I am enough as Barbara."

This shift in my life's context brings me joy and aliveness because I am putting my attention on being whole rather than on completing another project. Now, when daily I practice saying my commitments, I repeat both of my declarations. I am extending myself into the world.

Repeating the statements is necessary but insufficient. For them to be part of my being, I need to see a change in my actions. And I am. When Linda asked me to write this chapter, I had a series of excuses, or a story. It went like this: "I don't have a personal story that compares to those of the people we interviewed for this book and my writing style is different from yours."

Linda was patient and did not accept my excuses. Still, I procrastinated. Then, I read a meditation on grieving that made me recognize it was time to encapsulate the memories of my caring relationship with Ron. I embraced my learning edge and stepped forward. I have given myself permission to be free and vulnerable and to write about the generative foundational principles on which Ron and I designed and lived our friendship and partnership.

Being an observer of leadership is not enough. Practice is necessary to be a generative leader. It is not sufficient to read about cares, commitments, letting go, and being enough. It requires practice, and more practice—preferably with a community of fellow learners. Ron and I were one community of practice. Together we had conversations and made decisions based on our cares, we designed our vacations for fun, and we built time into each day and week to be together to strengthen our relationship.

Ron and I were also active learners in both the IGL and Strozzi learning communities. These communities provided a regular place to experiment, learn, and grow together. In these communities, we played together to sharpen our edges as individuals. This allowed each of us to fulfill our dreams and, in turn, guide leaders to achieve consistent results that create value for their customers. Bob Dunham's words sound in my head: "Don't fly solo." These places of practice have brought me into a new territory of learning, that of being part of a global world. Now I enter into conversations with these global leaders from a place of fascination. Together we support each other, in Bob Dunham's words, "to create a world in which everyone thrives."

We are all one in our learning.

APPRECIATIVE INQUIRY QUESTIONS TO PONDER

Discover

✓ What are the cares you are expressing in your family, community, and professional environment? How are you creating value in these areas that is observable, actionable, and recurrent?

Dream

✓ Share with family and friends your dream for increasing the effectiveness of your cares in your community or with customers.

Design

✓ What are different ways of expressing your commitment that will fulfill your cares?

Deliver

✓ Identify the roommate in your head. At least once today, when the roommate in your mind starts chattering, interrupt her/him and tell them what you care about. Continue this practice until the voice of the roommate grows quieter.

CHAPTER 3

This Is What I Am Supposed to Be Doing

DEANNA KOSARAJU WAS STRUGGLING WITH HER career choices. She had recently worked for the Anita Borg Institute (ABI) as the head of a successful program to hold Grace Hopper conferences in India. Her program had rapidly scaled to 5,000 attendees. Obviously, India's tech women were thirsty to be together and learn new information.

Despite this success, Deanna longed to create another conference, a "special" conference for Silicon Valley tech women. Unlike the Grace Hopper conference, which changed its city every year, this conference would be held annually near the heart of technology—San Francisco's South Bay area. ABI was committed to Grace Hopper and was, unfortunately, unable to provide support. Deanna was familiar with the tremendous effort it would take to start a new organization and bring her dream to reality. The money, the people, the publicity, the conference itself—the effort seemed almost impossible.

Deanna attended Women Leaders for the World (WLW) in 2012. She and all the other attendees had dreams. Several sessions focused on making their dreams seem more doable. They were exploring new ideas that would lead to their success. Deanna suddenly saw the way: she would make her organization *virtual*! Technologies were emerging that would allow hundreds of people to be part of an online conference. It would take a fraction of the effort, especially the funding. In 2012, online programs were rare. Deanna was going to be on the cutting edge of technology.

This idea changed the event's scope in another way: it could be global. The women she had worked with in India and many other countries could be part of the proceedings. She could draw on experts from around the world, not just the San Francisco Bay Area. With that realization, Global Tech Women was born.

As of 2021, there are 42,000 members of Global Tech Women on Facebook. In its sixth year of existence, the Women Transforming Technology seminar is expected to attract 10,000 attendees from around the world. Technology companies, lacking the ability to hold physical gatherings for their women employees due to the global pandemic, started jumping at the chance to sponsor the conference. They saw real value in being able to invite all their women employees, not just a privileged few. Many companies have global supply chains and global connections, and relationships are more important than ever.

Deanna is convinced she is "doing something right." Her gut tells her that "this is what I am supposed to be doing." She has a North Star guiding her. She feels that, like many of her fellow WLW grads, she is on the virtuous path. It was Aristotle who introduced the goal of development to be virtuous. In *Aristotle's Painful Path to Virtue* by Howard J. Curzer, he quotes Aristotle as saying, "We become just by performing just acts, and temperate by performing temperate acts."[21] Curzer goes on to say that virtuous path "means repeatedly doing the right thing" for the sake of doing it—not for personal rewards.

Deanna left the WLW program repeating her vision for the global conference over and over. At first, only a few people understood what she was talking about. She says she, "felt like a Broadway star from *Cats*—doing matinees and evening performances day after day." Finally, after many repetitions of her vision script, more and more people began getting the message.

Now Deanna is questioning what her real mission is. She muses, "Is my mission the conferences? Or are those merely a vehicle for building a global community?" She thinks that the truth is more about the community. She is building a solutions network on a global scale. People are becoming familiar with others who can help them solve what seem like intractable problems. She feels that her "global tech" women are putting the network to work in the way it is meant to be. The more people who join and participate, the more ripples in the pond.

The Personal Side

There was a deeper, more personal side to Deanna's understanding that confirmed she is doing what she is supposed to be doing. She says it was "a shift in my being that put me in touch with a center point of strength that I did not know I had." Over the last few years, she has met many role models who exhibited being well centered. Conscious practice brought out that quality in her. She credits that steady centeredness with guiding her through her struggles with breast cancer.

Her journey to beat the disease was riddled with ambiguity and uncertainty. Being centered helped her to take one day at a time and knowing her North Star gave her a much bigger future to live into.

In his book *Finite and Infinite Games*, James P. Carse postulates that there are two kinds of games in life. A finite game is one you play to win. An infinite game is one that you play to keep on playing. Deanna continually invents and wins many finite games. Every successful conference is a winning finite game through providing attendees with new skills and knowledge. These conferences are inside her bigger game of creating a worldwide solutions network of, and for, thousands of women.

As leaders, it is vital to find our North Stars and those of our teams. These guiding lights, these missions, can be found anywhere. In corporations, employees can truly believe in "putting a computer on every desk," "changing the trajectory of health for humanity," or some other worthy endeavor. They spend their time and energy (whether in support activities like human resources, finance, or facilities or on the front lines of research and engineering) fulfilling those missions.

In nonprofit organizations, people are passionate about "women leaders building nations" or "whole woman, whole leader, whole world." In our personal lives, we can make infinite commitments like "making this year the best year ever in my relationship with *(insert name)*," "exercising today to be able to exercise tomorrow," "saving energy everywhere I can to help our planet" or "living a joyful life." These commitments in our personal lives are important because they form the foundation for our careers and ability to contribute to others.

Even nations have North Stars expressed as "lift Nigerians out of poverty," "transforming India into a developed country," "being on the frontlines—fighting climate change, developing tomorrow's clean energy, driving economic growth and creating good jobs for Canadians."

APPRECIATIVE INQUIRY QUESTIONS TO PONDER

▥ *Discover*

✓ Do you have a guiding North Star? Is there an area in your life where you feel you are "doing the right thing"?

▥ *Dream*

✓ What is an infinite game you want to play?

▥ *Design*

✓ Create one or more finite games within that infinite game.

▥ *Deliver*

✓ Notice at least one time today when your North Star guided a decision you made.

CHAPTER 4

Passion and Love for Others

VALUES ARE A COMPASS THAT HELP guide decisions of good leaders and their teams. They are closely tied to what one cares about. They help set direction for a business, a community, an organization, a family, and a person. To begin our discussion of values, let us share this story about how one person's values led to the transformation of an African village.

In 2006, at age seventy-six, Mary Burns attended the Women Leaders for the World (WLW) program. Her vision focused on starting a school in Malawi. As she went through the class, those who interacted with her said they had never met anyone who so epitomized the word *love*. Soon after the class, Mary and her husband, Bob, founded the Kasimu Education Fund (KEF) to benefit the village of Manyessa, Malawi. Through KEF, a preschool was created. New school buildings were constructed. More teachers were trained. Educational grade levels were expanded so that children could complete their education and go on to university.

Kasimu Education Fund is an admirable model of sustainable development. Today, young men and women who are sent to university from the village learn to be teachers, medical technicians, and so on. They return to the village and give back so that others can follow in their footsteps. There is even a micro-lending operation so that educated young people have seed money to start their own businesses.

In 2009, Mary and her husband along with their son and granddaughter visited Manyessa. With his skills as a videographer, Mary's son, Patrick, captured the village's jubilation as the residents greeted the Burns family. The people in that village, as well as many others who met Mary, felt the love that had formed the foundation of her life. The year Mary died, she spoke at the United Nations about her work to improve lives in Malawi through education.

To give you an idea of how Mary Burns is remembered, the following is extracted from her 2014 obituary: "[She was] a passionate, loving, and feisty woman with a keen intelligence, she spent her life exploring spirituality, championing the underdog and seeking the divinity inherent in each of us." Anyone who knew Mary would tell you that she embodied passion and love for others with her indomitable spirit. Mary was a person who *lived* her values. Let's now look at some other examples.

Leading from Values

Dr. Barry Posner, former dean of the Leavey School of Business at Santa Clara University and well-known author of *The Leadership Challenge,* says that one of the five practices of successful leaders is having shared values. He not only writes about values but leads from them. In fact, shared values were a cornerstone of his time as the dean.

Barry values diversity. True to his value, he recruited several new female executive professors to draw on their years of success in the "real" world. When they joined his faculty, Barry had conversations with them about what they were passionate about and what they cared about. One of these new professors happened to be me (Linda). During a conversation with Barry, I expressed a desire to start a women's leadership center. Sometime later, Barry read an article in an educational magazine about the opening of a women's leadership center at a prestigious Eastern college. (He reads extensively and is always on the lookout for items of interest.) He saved the page, wrote in bold ink, "What do you think?" and mailed it to me.

After I read the article and Barry's note, I wrote back, "It's time!" That was the start of the Global Women's Leadership Network at Santa Clara University.

A Clash of Values

Maame Afon Yelbert-Sai was introduced in Chapter 1 as a junior member of Global Fund for Women (GFW). In 2011, she joined a young organization called Women's Earth Alliance (WEA) as the Africa program director. She loved the challenges of the position, which included:

+ To grow the African program through resource mobilization.

+ To build an advisory council.

+ To make the program robust.

+ To cultivate relevant and strategic partnerships.

Here was a place where she could make the audacious decisions that she felt ready to make. Here was an environment where her passion for social justice and international development would be welcomed and intersect. Every ounce of her being wanted to make sure that African women got resources, respect, and an opportunity for their dreams to become reality. She wanted the solutions to come from local expertise. Americans (of any color or country of origin) did not have the right to tell their African counterparts what to do or how to do it. She was committed that it will not be business as usual.

Maame would soon be disappointed by a clash with her values, however. Ahead of a trip to Liberia and Sierra Leone—a trip that eventually got canceled—she was brimming with the ideas that would allow her to live these values. However, as a result of opposing priorities, and with the trip canceled, those ideas were cut off. Further, as she hired two African women as interns, her decisions were questioned. Maame seemed to have hit a wall in the organization and the ensuing consequence was her parting ways with it.

She stepped away from WEA into reflection—deep reflection. Her faith and prayer helped her through this time. She saw a journey ahead for herself—one of service and stewardship. She poured herself into missions that aligned with her values. In particular, she became a leader within the African Women's Development Fund, USA (AWDF USA).

She awoke to the idea that hope and courage are contagious. So are joy and humor. Her mission was to tap into her energy and spread it around the world. She would no longer hold herself back. Her spark would light others' sparks. By seeing one woman with a voice and in congruence with her values, other people would find their own voices.

Maya Angelou's famous quote, "I've learned that people will forget what you said, people will forget what you did, but people will never forget how you made them feel," became a guiding light for Maame. She wanted everyone she encountered to feel heard, valued, and welcomed.

Maame is a proud African woman. She is proud to be Black. She honors who she is. She is teaching her children to embody those values, too.

Value Defined

What is a value? Brené Brown in *Dare to Lead* defines a value as "A way of being or believing that you hold most important."[22] Chapter 1 explored finding out what you care about. What you care about is closely associated with the values you hold most dear.

The first step in being able to live from values is knowing what they are. There are many lists of values that one could use to select words that represent inner guiding lights. Explore the Internet and find a list that resonates with you. You may want to find a list in your first language if non-English words have more meaning to you.

Being clear about our values may seem like a simple exercise. It is trickier than it looks to discern a value that was *freely* chosen versus one that was "embedded" by family, tribe, religion, country, etc. Take the value "hard work," for instance. Almost by definition, if you were born in the United States, you value hard work. It is a basic premise of the Puritan ethic.

So, was one taught that hard work is the way to live or was it freely chosen?

Americans who value "freedom" might want to ask whether that value was chosen or embedded in them as a foundation of "the American way." Those who value "politeness" would want to consider whether that's an aspect of their culture (like it is in Japan), or is it a reflection of their true nature? Those who value "community" might inquire whether that value originates in being part of a tribe.

After careful reflection, you can identify several values you personally chose and that, along with those embedded in you, form the foundation of your belief system.

The second step in living from values is to examine how congruent your behavior is with those beliefs and then finding ways to be more aligned with them. If good health is what you value, are you getting enough exercise? Eating the right foods? Observing any doctor-directed monitoring like taking your blood pressure every day? If family or love is a value, how much time do you spend with your spouse, kids, parents, or siblings? If learning is a value, how often do you find yourself on the learning edge—trying new approaches?

Once you have examined how congruent you are with your values, you can initiate new actions if required. For instance, you can choose to join a gym, play soccer with the kids, or adopt a new hobby.

Finally, leaders who are interested in becoming more effective can choose a value to be practiced, internalized, and mastered. Their organization may be trying to launch partnerships, so they choose to be more collaborative. Or it may be trying to penetrate markets in other countries, so they need to adopt a global view. Or their business needs to be more entrepreneurial, so they decide to concentrate on innovation.

Values in Today's World

Businesses today are going through a transition as the baby boomers retire and the younger generations take charge of the organizations. In general, the younger generations are interested in more than a job, particularly millennials. They want to believe in what their organizations stand for. They want to know what the values of their companies are.

Values are an invisible force in corporate cultures, having explicit discussions about them can bring clarity. Sometimes, change is stimulated through such exercises or by exterior pressures—even legislation. The need for change has become visible in the world of technology with employees from companies such as Facebook and Google questioning the actions of their organizations.

Values permeate our society. For instance, they appear to have played an important part in the COVID-19 crisis. As of the end of 2020, the United States represented only 4 percent of the world's population, yet it suffered nearly a quarter of the world's deaths. Why? The research of a Dutch social psychologist, Geert Hofstede, may hold a clue to the reason. Hofstede originally identified four cultural dimensions. One of these was what he termed *individualism/collectivism,* and among the most individualistic societies in the world is the United States. In an article entitled "National Culture" on the Hofstede Insights website the terms are defined as follows:

The high side of this dimension, called Individualism, can be defined as a preference for a loosely knit social framework in which individuals are expected to take care of only themselves and their immediate families.

Its opposite, Collectivism, represents a preference for a tightly knit framework in society in which individuals can expect their relatives or members of a particular ingroup to look after them in exchange for unquestioning loyalty. A society's position on this dimension is reflected in whether people's self-image is defined in terms of "I" or "we."[23]

During the COVID-19 crisis, the "social good" of lockdowns, mask wearing, social distancing, and even life-saving vaccinations confronted the strongly embedded value of independence. This values clash was reinforced by a strong political divide. The results are history: Many people died. The power of values to influence actions cannot be denied at both the individual and collective level.

Appreciative Inquiry Questions to Ponder

▨ *Discover*

✓ Complete the exercise mentioned in this chapter to find your personal values. Now think about your organization and its values. Look for the congruence of your personal and organizational values.

✓ Look at each personal value you selected. Did you freely choose it?

▨ *Dream*

✓ Imagine ways that by living from your values they can help you move forward with ease and grace in your life and/or your leadership.

▨ *Design*

✓ Think of ways that you can become more (fill in a value you chose from the list). How will you know that you are leading from that value?

▨ *Deliver*

✓ Have a conversation with your team about the organization's values and their personal ones. Look for alignment. What did you learn from that conversation?

PART TWO

Vision and Commitment

CHAPTER 5

One Million More Babies to Loving Homes

VISIONS SUCH AS GANDHI'S "FREE INDIA" have changed millions of lives. Can only "grand" visions be life-changing? Absolutely not. Is there a role for vision in our personal and everyday professional lives? Absolutely! While a personal vision may not affect millions of people, millions of like-minded visions, when considered collectively, *can* have a major impact. Let's explore the power of one's vision when it is strongly connected to what one cares about.

Vision Creates Reality

Sandhya Puchalapalli is an Indian woman who lives in Kadapa. Her city is part of the state of Andra Kadesh in the south central part of India. It is a fascinating country on so many levels—historical, religious, ecological diversity, cuisine, etc., but it does have its downside. As a country, India is the seventh largest by area, sixth largest economy ($2.6 trillion) and second largest by population at 1.2 billion people. Its economy is growing rapidly, but the Gross Domestic Product per capita is a low $1,940. It has the largest number of people living below the World Bank poverty level of $1.25 per day.

An estimated 6.8 million fewer female births will be recorded across India by 2030 because of the persistent use of selective abortions, researchers estimate.[24] Sandhya speaks of female infanticide in broad terms. She points out that like most male-dominated cultures, Indian families prefer male children. The dowry—a cultural practice outlawed in 1961 but still observed—exacerbates the preference. The dowry is paid by the girl's parents to the groom to supposedly support their daughter as part of a new family. It is the equivalent of one year's income for many poor families. The stark reality is that the daughter can become almost an unpaid slave to her mother-in-law in her new home. Her statements are borne out in numerous articles, including one entitled "Girls Interrupted."[25]

With new technologies such as ultrasound, many baby girls are aborted, and others just left to die after birth. In some cases, it is not the dowry that is the root cause of these actions. As hard as it seems to believe, some Indian mothers just do not want their daughters to have the same wretched life that they have had. A 2018 article on the website Humanium.org states, "The United Nations recently declared India to be the world's most dangerous place for girls: Until the age of five, according to a new UN study, their mortality rate is 75 percent higher than that of boys."[26]

About twenty years ago, Sandhya started taking in unwanted, abandoned children because they touched her heart. Her American nieces had raised $501 and sent it to her. From this inauspicious start, Aarti Home was born—named for her niece Aarti who died during the home's first years. One thing Aarti Home taught Sandhya is that 90 percent of India's abandoned children are girls.

With more than 1,000 children passing through its doors, Aarti Home has become a haven for those who have suffered abuse, trafficking, and abandonment. One of our friends who has visited there, Abha Singhvi, says it is one of the most "loving places on earth."

In 2007, as president of the Vijay Foundation Trust (Aarti Home), Sandhya attended the Women Leaders for the World (WLW) program in the United States. She wanted to double the size of her orphanage. As she attended the classes and walked the beautiful trails of the California foothills, she connected more deeply with her passion. She saw new possibilities beyond her orphanage. She fashioned a vision: to have 1 million more girls go home from the hospital to loving families.

With this vision in mind, she began taking new actions when she returned home. She broadened her work to address the underlying gender discrimination and violence affecting both women and girls. She enlisted gynecologists to not reveal the sex of babies shown in various tests. She counseled women to deliver their babies before deciding to give them up for adoption. Today, her work aims to help women achieve economic and emotional independence, gain confidence, and understand their personal rights.

What has her vision coupled with her energy and compassion accomplished? More than 30,000 women have been trained in leadership, a vocation, or employable skills. Her three-month intensive vocational training programs have been attended by more than 20,000 formerly destitute women. The female:male ratio has even improved slightly in the last few years.[27]

Sandhya is not a lone example of the power of vision. Nor is she the only one for whom a retreat to nature provided the stimulus for the next chapter of life.

Guiding Lights to Create a Vision

You do not have to have an epiphany to formulate a vision, nor do you need advertising-worthy wording. Another way to create a vision is to craft a commitment and see where it leads you. Here are some common commitments that shape actions:

✦ *I will believe in myself.*

✦ *I will seek guidance from God or a higher power.*

✦ *I will be adaptable and flexible.*

✦ *I will stay on my learning edge.*

✦ *I will help the children in my life build their visions.*

✦ *I will make every year the best one in my relationship with (insert name).*

✦ *I will support my community's effort to (fill in the blank).*

Some popular books can help you craft general commitments. One worth reading is Don Miguel Ruiz's best-selling book *The Four Agreements*. Based on Toltec wisdom, it espouses commitments (agreements) that free adherents from their self-limiting beliefs. When voluntarily adopted as ways of living, they, too, can be guiding lights. The Four Agreements are:

1. Be impeccable with your word.

2. Do not take anything personally.

3. Do not make assumptions.

4. Always do your best.[28]

Visons can arise from commitments like these—for example, perhaps your vision becomes that you want your organization to be known for its integrity. Ruiz's first three commitments are foundational agreements for making this happen, and the fourth ensures that you will make your best efforts. Or perhaps your vision is harmony at home. All Four Agreements could apply there as well.

Many charitable organizations paint a picture with their visions of the impact their organization is devoted to creating. Here are a few examples:

✦ African Library Project: "Placing books in the hands of the young—like dropping seeds onto good, watered soil."[29]

✦ She-Can: "Educate a woman, change a nation."[30]

✦ We Care Solar: "We light every birth."[31]

The National Bonner Leaders Program at Virginia Wesleyan University has six commitments for its graduates that can translate into one's personal vision or a collective vision:

✦ **Civic Engagement:** We participate intentionally as a citizen in the democratic process, actively engaging in public policy and direct services.

✦ **Community Building:** We establish and sustain a vibrant community of place, personal relationships, and common interests.

✦ **Diversity:** We respect and embrace the many dimensions of diversity in our private and public lives.

✦ **International Perspective:** We develop international understanding that enables us to participate successfully in a global society.

✦ **Spiritual Exploration:** We explore personal belief while respecting the spiritual practices of others.

✦ **Social Justice:** We advocate for fairness, impartiality, and equity while addressing systemic social and environmental issues.[32]

Sometimes visions can be represented in beautiful pictures and songs. Barbra Streisand performed her vision for the world in 2016, which you can watch on YouTube by searching: "Barbra Streisand—Pure Imagination (Live 2016)." We've heard that Barbara Streisand was once asked, "Should I be an actor?" and she responded, "Only if you are passionate about acting." Like Streisand's passion for singing, acting, and directing, the best visions lead to devotion. They lead to something you cannot *not* do.

APPRECIATIVE INQUIRY QUESTIONS TO PONDER

▦ Discover

✓ What vision did you have for your life when you were a teenager? What about in your twenties, thirties, and beyond?

✓ What commitments have you made about your family? Your health? Your financial well-being?

▦ Dream

✓ What is your vision now?

▦ Design

✓ What practices can you adopt that are most conducive to the fulfillment of your vision?

▦ Deliver

✓ What step will you take this week toward your vision?

CHAPTER 6

One Computer
for the Library

WE THINK THAT WE ARE ALWAYS MOVING forward into the future. Our eyes being positioned on the front of our face are one cause for that illusion. So, we logically conclude that we are moving that way and thinking that way. Our brains, however, have a million filters from the past that color our thinking about what is ahead and even about what is possible. When we break free from some of those filters, it can fuel progress from hopelessness to hope—as individuals and as leaders. The following story about Alma Cota de Yanez illustrates the concept of freeing oneself from limiting filters.

Taking on the Near Impossible

Nogales, Sonora, Mexico, is a poor town perched on the border between Mexico and the United States. At all hours of the day and night, trains hurry north and south through the center of town carrying parts and finished products to and from the manufacturing plants (called *maquiladoras* or twin plants). Houses and hovels pepper the hillsides of mountains on either side of the narrow pass. When the torrential rains come—as monsoons do every summer—the main street floods dividing the city.

The passage of the North American Free Trade Agreement (NAFTA) in 1994 prompted rapid expansion of the *maquiladoras* near Nogales—attracting desperate workers from across Mexico to the new jobs. Low wages, after all, are better than no wages. With the workers came their families, so between 1990 and 2000 the population mushroomed by 50 percent. Today, the population is approaching 300,000. The few government-supplied social services are stretched beyond their limits. Adding to the burden of caring for an impoverished population are the thousands of deportees dumped into Nogales by the U.S. government each year.

In 2005, a young woman from Nogales, Alma Cota de Yanez, applied for the inaugural class of the Women Leaders for the World (WLW) program in California. She was the head of a charity named Fundación Del Empresariado Sonorense, A.C. (FESAC). Her mission was to help ten small nonprofits try to alleviate the problems caused by the rapid growth. In her application, she described herself as a hardworking, lonely woman with a coffee pot and a copier. This was her image of herself—from her background of being raised in the Hispanic culture where women are traditionally not the leaders in the community.

The project she proposed working on (which she saw as nearly impossible at the time) was to obtain *one* computer for the library. That computer would enable the charities she assisted to apply for much-needed funding using the Internet. She compared not having computer access to "driving a horse-drawn carriage on a U.S. freeway." Even one computer could be a way out of scarcity and hopelessness.

At that point, her definition of the word *vision* was "something that you inscribed on your tombstone"—like "Here lies Alma, a woman who aspired to do good." What Alma discovered as she attended the leadership class was that vision is like a lighthouse for your life. It is the compass that helps to steer the boat. She fell in love with one of the visioning exercises— the top of the mountain. She put her vision for having well-funded Nogales non-governmental organizations (NGOs) able to aid numerous people on the apex. The computer was an immediate goal on the way to that vision. She created many different pathways to obtain the machine.

When she returned to Nogales, she was on fire with a passion to bring computer access to her followers. The lonely individual with the coffee pot and copier became the Red Lipstick leader. (On days when she needed extra courage, she put on the brightest color she could find.)

An organization in Arizona was "refreshing" their office computers. They would gift ten machines to FESAC. Now how could Alma get them across the border? Who did she have to be to bring them into Mexico under the eyes of the customs agency?

She put on her bright red lipstick, summoned up her courage, and went to meet with the head of the customs agency. As she related her story to the manager, he became an ally. Soon, she had the computers in Nogales, Sonora, Mexico—without going to jail. Little did she know at the time, but cross-border partnerships were going to become an important part of her and FESAC's future.

Be careful what you wish for—her computer journey had just begun. Obtaining the physical computers was just a start. None of the NGO volunteers knew how to turn them on or how to compose an email. A local vocational high school offered to teach basic skills. The fifty-plus-year-old homemakers went back to school. By Christmas time, they were happily printing holiday cards to send from each of their organizations.

Alma had succeeded; the NGOs were connected to the Internet. Communications improved, and they started working as a team to increase their community impact. Their newfound computer skills broke them out of isolation. Together, they had become a network.

Alma had left the lonely woman leader identity behind. She had become the Red Lipstick leader—a master at networking, visioning, and breaking free from the limited thinking of the past.

There are several parts of Alma's story that illustrate breaking with the past. She took on a challenge that was possible but almost unimaginable given her current self-assessment. Access for all the people served by her charities was something she truly cared about. The challenge called forth new approaches, the courage to overcome fears, and stretching beyond what she thought she was capable of.

Let's look now at a step-by-step process for breaking free.

Breaking Free

RISK is a simple four-step method for breaking free from the past. It stands for **R**ecognize, **I**dentify, **S**hift, **K**now. The four steps are focused on the unexplored stories from our past, particularly those that no longer serve us and that are holding us back from our full potential.

We define a *story* as a description—either true or imagined—of a connected series of events. There is no story that tells exactly what went on from all points of view. There is no *one,* true story—only many points of view. These stories have their origins in our culture, history, language, religions, countries, family, etc. Those from factors closest to us like from our family are called proximal. These have the strongest grip on us.

Stories can be interpreted as positive or negative. Either kind can be limiting, precluding us from taking certain actions, sapping our energy, influencing our values, and limiting our thinking. The RISK method is designed to give us freedom to act in a new way. Here are the steps:

1. **R**ecognize is to become aware of the story. This can be a sudden awakening or occur gradually over time.

2. **I**dentify it as a "story." Naming it helps to distinguish it. If we can see an incident that might have set it in motion, that is particularly useful.

3. **S**hift the story. If that story is not true, what is possible? If the story involved being hurt, we try to forgive the person. Fred Luskin, an authority on forgiveness, says it "means the decision to free us from the personal offense and blame that has us stuck in a cycle of suffering."[33] The act of forgiving brings us peace of mind. We take responsibility for how we are feeling about the story. We shift, perhaps, from blaming to forgiveness. This step gives us separation from the story.

4. Know that the stories that have had power over us will return. Every time they do, we have an opportunity to quickly recognize their recurrence, reidentify it, and shift it again. Eventually, through practice, the process can become almost instantaneous. We can say, "Oh, there is that old story again!" At that point, we have more choice about our actions. They are free from that past incident.

Applying the four-step RISK process allows you to step into who you are becoming. What might look hopeless when gripped by our past stories or our choice of words may become possible through a shift in the context.

APPRECIATIVE INQUIRY QUESTIONS TO PONDER

Discover

✓ What is a story that is limiting you? Name it.

Dream

✓ What would life look like if that story did not exist?

Design

✓ Create a skit that pokes fun at the story—the funnier the better.

Deliver

✓ What one action can you take today to move away from the limitations of that story?

CHAPTER 7

A Disruptive Transformational Vision

THE WORD *DISRUPTIVE* SUGGESTS groundbreaking innovation. Our lifetimes have seen the introduction of many disruptive technologies. Some recent ones include the Internet, GPS, artificial intelligence, and digital photography. Such disruptive technologies change whole industries and the pattern of our lives. They sweep away inferior solutions and replace them with those that are far superior. The same is true of a disruptive transformational vision.

What happens when a group of healthcare companies rethink the very foundation of their industry? What becomes possible when they shift their focus from only curing illnesses to also focusing on prevention measures that create healthier lives and communities? This story looks at the importance of individuals, teams, organizations, and whole industries identifying and initiating actions in concert with a disruptive transformational vision. It highlights the importance of processes that engage a diversity of stakeholders in conversations that create collective action. These actions include making commitments, plans, and decisions that consider the cares of companies, communities, and government. Teams and organizations that take coordinated action, based on systems thinking, increase their results and their impact. Let's start with the story of one person who led during this revolution in the healthcare industry.

A Place for Self-Expression

Kathryn Johnson is an American who graduated in political science from Indiana University and obtained a master's in Organizational Development from Boston University. She devoted twenty-five years of her life to leading an organization called the Health Forum. In the years that Kathryn worked there, the Health Forum grew from a regional organization to a global one. The company offered communications, information, education, and research products and services for healthcare leaders. At the core of the Health Forum was a dedication to a vision of "creating healthier communities." People could live longer and have a better quality of life if their communities placed a higher emphasis on prevention.

Most of the health industry in the 1980s was focused on sickness and illness. Kathryn knew she had to build a vision at the Health Forum that was shared by her senior team, and even her board of directors. It would take years to enroll enough healthcare leaders and their teams in taking a new direction that could result in large-scale systems change. She needed innovative ideas and processes. She would need the assistance of experts in the field of visioning and collective action.

Over the years, Kathryn and the Health Forum engaged those experts who helped them to launch:

- ✦ Vision Quest—a series of three-day retreats with twenty invitees from leading health and health-related associations. Organizations like AARP, the Healthcare Manufacturers Association, the AMA, and the American Nursing Association did not just send anyone to participate. They invited their board members and CEOs to be part of these important conversations. As a result of the first session, fifteen organizations changed their vision statements to include healthier communities. The business leaders in particular saw that stimulating health systems would result in their own companies being healthier—providing services and impacting profitability.

- ✦ A Healthier Communities Fellowship program to engage people from all fields in healthcare discussions. The first of these fellowship programs was attended by mayors, city managers, and heads of school systems as well as influential community leaders. The program has had more than 2,000 graduates.

- ✦ A Healthier Communities Award program and an Annual Healthier Communities Summit that recognized multiple levels of best practices in the industry in the United States and beyond.

- ✦ A series of publications that featured articles about healthy communities.

- ✦ Learning collaboratives that brought together a consortium of healthcare organizations, including major global players like the World Health Organization (WHO), to find synergies.

✦ A Leadership Center that engaged a panel of blue-chip advisors such as renowned authors of leadership books and luminaries in that field such as Rosa Beth Moss Kanter, Peter Drucker and Jim Collins.

Through these programs, Kathryn and Healthcare Forum gained a reputation as leaders and innovators. Gradually, all types of healthcare organizations shifted their focus to broader social determinants of health and well-being. Shared, well-grounded visions last decades. Contained in these healthcare institutions are commitments to communities beyond providing medical services:

✦ Cleveland Clinic—"Community: *We are committed to the communities we serve.* Cleveland Clinic's community benefit goes beyond healthcare services. As an anchor institution, we promote the physical and economic health of our neighborhoods. We are building a future for health education and workforce development that will enhance the region for generations."[34]

✦ Duke Health—"In *advancing health together,* we will:
  • Deliver tomorrow's health care today
  • Accelerate discovery and its translation
  • Create education that is transforming
  • Build healthy communities
  • Connect with the world to improve health globally"[35]

✦ Kaiser Permanente—"Our vision at Kaiser Permanente is to be a leader in total health by making lives better."[36]

✦ Bon Secours Health System—"Inspired by God's hope for the world, we will be a ministry where associates want to work, clinicians want to practice, people seek wellness and communities thrive."[37]

Vision as a North Star

On a personal level, Kathryn utilized her vision for healthier communities as a compass for her decision-making. As CEO, she sought board members for their reputation as innovators. There was a thirst for outliers—people who were futurists and disruptors. The same was true for staff and even in the selection of strategic partnerships. A fundamental alignment around building well-being into all aspects of community life was at the base of decision-making. Kathryn identified leaders across sectors to expand and create communities whose focus was greater than the traditional health model.

Their "true north" orientation also opened interesting opportunities. Health Forum, unlike many nonprofit organizations, had revenue streams outside of membership dues, conferences, and donations. Their corporate partnerships raised millions of dollars to sponsor the awards, fellowships, etc. Employees, board members, and interns were attracted because they wanted to work with these changemakers. After their graduation, the Health Forum Fellows spread out across all aspects of the healthcare industry and today are major leaders in the field.

At her farewell dinner, Kathryn expressed her feelings of joy at seeing the vision of healthier communities becoming mainstream and many of her fellow Health Forum leaders were viewed as disrupters of the status quo. Kathryn's story demonstrates a leader who was motivated by a vision to make lasting impact on the lives and health of communities everywhere.

Kathryn continues to help build healthy communities. This time, communities of women working to make the world a better place. She was a dedicated board member of the Global Women's Leadership Network, which sponsored the Women Leaders for the World program for many years.

APPRECIATIVE INQUIRY QUESTIONS TO PONDER

▦ *Discover*

✓ For the next week, at least once per day, ask someone in your life (family, organization, community), to tell you about a dream they have for the future.

▦ *Dream*

✓ Choose one problem in your life, company, team, or community. Instead of focusing on that problem, craft a disruptive, transformational vision about it.

▦ *Design*

✓ What would your life, company, team, or community look like when that vision is even partially fulfilled? How would you feel about life, etc. when that progress is made?

▦ *Deliver*

✓ With your disruptive, transformational vision as the basis for your "true north," plan the three to five steps that will carry you toward it.

CHAPTER 8

I Will Not Grow Old Without Making a Difference

Barbara Bylenga, founder, and executive director of SHE-CAN, believes that talented young women, especially those from post-conflict countries, should be able to obtain an excellent education. They should be able to build a foundation for life that would allow them to be leaders in organizations, communities, and the world.

Here is how a recent SHE-CAN grant proposal describes the issue:

> Women are severely underrepresented at all levels of leadership and decision-making worldwide. Lack of female representation has had direct impact on the well-being of societies and people. Female leadership in the public as well as the private sector is crucial for the betterment of societies, and the creation of more inclusive policies and opportunities for all women.
>
> While significant efforts to advance women have been made, representation has not increased in a decade. In terms of power and decision making, women held only

28% of managerial positions globally in 2019—almost the same proportion as in 1995.[38]

Women need more than basic education and an income to influence high-level decision-making. Their peers (and for elected officials, voters) need to view them as credible which often means having higher education and technical knowledge.[39]

Key barriers need to be addressed. Young women, especially young women from developing countries, face significant barriers to attaining higher education. They lack college preparation (i.e., quality English preparation and secondary education) that male and wealthy peers are more likely to be able to access. They also lack exposure to 1) women role models who show them they can become women with power in their societies, 2) networks that will connect them to influential positions, and 3) the soft skills that allow them to successfully navigate higher levels of the socio-economic pyramid.[40]

The need was clear to Barbara. She saw women having been severely underrepresented at all decision-making tables globally, going back centuries, and it was clear to her that the world has suffered because of that. She would start a nonprofit (then called Open A Door) that would focus on raising money for undergraduate scholarships, with the first recipients being from Rwanda.[41]

Attending the Leadership Program

In 2012, Barbara, a former trend researcher, met Kathryn Johnson (featured in Chapter 7). As a board member for Global

Women's Leadership Network (GWLN), Kathryn was always recruiting for the annual leadership program. During their first luncheon conversation, Kathryn urged Barbara to attend it.

Barbara listened, accepted the invitation, and even convinced her chief financial officer, Carol Chang, to go with her. The pair would explore what Open A Door, a one-year-old organization, could become. Barbara says that she really did not know what she wanted for Open A Door. What she did know is that she did not want to grow old as a trend researcher, and instead she "wanted to make a difference." She had a strong urge to do something, but what? Alongside uncertainty was a fear of failure—what if she left no legacy! Something in her drove her forward. The "universe" was sending her on a virtuous path to Women Leaders for the World (WLW).

Each class spends one evening preparing for a presentation to the GWLN community. They are asked to share their vision for their organization and an inspiring challenge they will be working toward in the coming year.

Barbara recalls struggling to find the words. Everyone else was feeling lighthearted and started to party. Barbara hung back to think more deeply. Finally, she saw that her vision was to build global women's leadership. Those educated women would rebuild nations. Today, those words have morphed into a strong statement of intention: *Supporting **H**er Education— Changes **A** Nation* and, in 2014, the name of the organization was officially changed to SHE-CAN!

Since 2011, SHE-CAN has helped seventy-four women win full-ride, four-year scholarships totaling over $19 million. In 2021, thirty-nine young women are studying in U.S. universities and colleges from Rwanda, Liberia, and Cambodia.

Thirty-five others have college degrees. SHE-CAN expanded into Guatemala in 2021, and their first Guatemalan scholars will begin college in the United States in 2023.

What Were the Keys to Success?

If you are going to award scholarships, you need to raise money, and Barbara was a novice at that task. Fortunately, she found a real expert to help—Julie Abrams. Over the next seven years, Julie worked with Barbara as a paid consultant, bringing a strong voice in shaping the business model and building a network. She credits Julie with teaching her how to establish and grow the non-profit.

There were five components to the business model that Barbara developed:

1. **Focus on post-conflict nations**, those that are recovering from war or genocide. They believe these countries truly need women leaders, and therefore, the impact will be most significant.

2. **Identify low-income women,** those who excel academically and show strong leadership potential, through extensive, in-person recruiting trips to their countries. By only accepting low-income women and helping them leapfrog into leadership positions, they believe they are not just building women's leadership but also addressing the severe income divide that plagues these nations.

3. **Invite prominent colleges and universities to provide funding for tuition, room, and board**. Focus on those who

want the best and the brightest low-income young women but are unable to identify them through their recruiting process. It is unusual for some of these U.S. universities to award full scholarships to international students, but this was about adding talented diversity, both socio-economic and cultural, to their campuses.

4. **Match each scholar with a team of five U.S. professionals** who support her in preparing for and winning a scholarship. Then, these same mentors continue to support her throughout her four years at university by providing emotional support, a place to stay on holidays and valuable career-building connections. They continue to give advice as the graduates launch their careers back home. The mentorship program allows SHE-CAN to capture the intense desire many U.S. people have to personally help a young woman with high potential, and directly address the problem of low representation of women leaders around the globe.

5. **Support each scholar's out-of-pocket costs**, those not covered by their university scholarship by requiring each mentor to donate $1,000 per year to their scholar in the program. Their donations cover scholars' pre-college exam preparation, immigration documents, plane tickets, dorm supplies, winter clothes, books, health insurance, computer, phone, etc.

Today, nine universities consistently offer SHE-CAN scholarships each year and there are four more who do it occasionally. Over 400 U.S. professionals support scholars as mentors. Another sixty are part of the SHE-CAN volunteer corps named Power to Fly. All share their wisdom and expertise with scholars through short-term projects. The business model, with its five key components, has provided a solid foundation for scaling the work of SHE-CAN.

Breaking the Back of Cultural Suppression

Barbara likes to tell the story of a young woman from Cambodia, Phalkun Out, who was selected on an initial recruiting trip. She was the eleventh highest scorer out of 90,000 students who took the country's National Exam that year. Now, Barbara was visiting to provide this young woman and three others who would come to the United States with an orientation about the SHE-CAN program they were entering.

During orientation, Barbara was stopped dead in her tracks when Phalkun asked this question, "Why should women be leaders?" She believed that despite her academic achievements, she should just bear children and take care of a family. Her cultural heritage would have denied her a future she deserved. Barbara responded with facts about the contributions that women were capable of making outside the home and how Cambodian society could benefit by having women in leadership positions.

And what has happened to Phalkun since that conversation about women as leaders? She graduated from Lafayette College with an engineering management degree in 2020. She is now a Clean Energy Ambassador for a large multinational company, Energy Nexus. Through in-person and media-training programs, she is influencing millions of people. Phalkun is involved in helping Cambodians deliver water, energy, and food in a sustainable and equitable way. What a loss it would have been if she had not been supported by SHE-CAN.

Why Women Leaders?

Developments during the global epidemic demonstrated the efficacy of women as leaders. An International Leadership Association article from August 2020 states, "Comprising only some 8 percent of political leaders globally, women have accounted for an estimated 40 percent of the most successful responses to COVID-19! *New York Times* columnist Nicholas Kristof's comparative analysis pointed out that women-led countries have a six-times lower death rate than those led by male counterparts in similar countries."[42] Those women leaders from Denmark, Finland, Germany, Iceland, New Zealand, Norway, and Taiwan are not superhuman. What they did was simple, but courageous. They listened to the scientists, took the pandemic seriously, were decisive, and showed empathy. Their actions saved lives.

John Gerzema, CEO of The Harris Poll, is a pioneer in the use of data to identify social change. He and his coauthor, Michael D'Antonio, wrote *The Athena Doctrine*[43] based on a worldwide study of 64,000 people. The book's subtitle is *How Women (and the Men Who Think Like Them) Will Rule the Future*.

There were two parts to their research effort. First, they asked people to name the characteristics they wanted in their leaders for the twenty-first century. Once these were compiled, they asked a second, independent group of people whether those characteristics were more "masculine" or "feminine." The results overwhelmingly showed that people are seeking leaders with more "feminine" tendencies.

Among the characteristics people wanted in their leaders, and which were considered "feminine" were:

+ Expressive   + Intuitive

+ Passionate   + Collaborative

+ Selfless

Among those that people did not correlate with modern leadership and which they thought were more "masculine" were:

+ Aggressive   + Independent

+ Analytic   + Proud

Barbara Bylenga and those who support SHE-CAN want to ensure that countries like Rwanda, Cambodia, Liberia, and Guatemala have well-educated, capable women leaders who can contribute their unique female perspective to high-level decision making. SHE-CAN is a success because the founders are passionate about their mission and because they built a strong business model to sustain their organization.

APPRECIATIVE INQUIRY QUESTIONS TO PONDER

Discover
✓ Can you identify an "urge" to take a virtuous path?

Dream
✓ What would the world look like if you followed that path and were successful?

Design
✓ What are the key elements to a business model that would make it possible to fulfill that path?

Deliver
✓ Talk to a friend or advisor about your virtuous path and the aspects of your prospective business model you like the most.

PART THREE

Listening and Questioning

CHAPTER 9

Listening with an Empty Head

How a person chooses to listen is one way to shift the context of their life. When a leader directs their listening, they can better foster cultures of creativity and openness. Listening more deeply for the essence of what is being said gives us real power to shift a situation. As you will see, it creates "power with" instead of "power over." Dr. Florence Temu, country director of the African Medical and Research Foundation (AMREF) Tanzania, is a leader who listens in this way.

The United Nations estimated Tanzania's 2018 population at 56.31 million, which is slightly smaller than South Africa, making it the second most populous country located entirely south of the Equator. The population is composed of about 120 ethnic, linguistic, and religious groups. One may anticipate that such diversity may complicate the work of organizations such as AMREF, but fortunately, the Kiswahili language (the national language of Tanzania) has made it easier for communities from different parts of the country to communicate.

Returning to her country after the Women Leaders for the World (WLW) program in 2017, Florence was on a mission.

The young people in her country, even college graduates, had few employment opportunities. Florence knew that, in many cases, they were resigned to or even resentful of their predicament. She wanted to turn their negative attitudes into ambition and, ultimately, to employment. Let's talk about how she accomplished this turnaround.

Listening to Others

Florence started listening to truly hear where the young people's ideas originated. She says that she went with an "empty head" and started with an open mind—one that is free of judgment. It was Rumi who said, "The quieter you become the more you are able to hear." Indeed, when you sit silently the messages you receive will become clearer.

A bounty of ideas emerged from the conversations when she listened this way. The ideas morphed into discussions of pros and cons. Eventually, clarity, focus, and action emerged.

Florence found it is easier to have conversations when she did not expect other people to have the same ideas she had. She found that her new way of listening gave her energy and also brought it to others. They felt heard. They trusted her more when she was aligning with their ideas rather than trying to sell her own approaches. She says that even when their idea was not the one selected, they displayed more confidence.

Her listening created safe spaces in which others could express themselves. It encouraged others to put aside their grievances and frustrations and begin to dream. Florence has dedicated herself (until her retirement) to helping these young people and her junior staff reach their dreams.

Automatic Listening
Versus Listening for Agreement

Florence shifted her listening. Accomplishing this requires an awareness of normal listening habits and an effort to consciously direct our listening to be open-minded and nonjudgmental. Normal listening (aka automatic listening) is the way we have been listening all our lives. Listening is a combination of hearing and the intellectual component of understanding. It is an ingrained human capability. For example, one way the intellectual component can come into play is to listen for whether we agree with what is being said. Can you hear yourself doing that right now? *Do I agree that how we listen is an ingrained human capability? Do I listen for agreement?*

The intellectual part of listening makes a lot of judgments about what is being said: *Is this right or is this wrong? Is this good or is this bad? Do I like it, or do I not like it? Does it fit with my point of view?* In a business meeting, do you hear yourself asking, "Do we have budget for this?" Or "Will this really work?" Or are you trying to formulate your own response instead of spending time understanding? Do you work with someone whose response is often, "Let me play the devil's advocate"? It is not the devil making that person look at the negative side of a topic. It is the way they listen: to find what is wrong. Using the expression "devil's advocate" legitimizes their critique.

Is it possible to shift the way we listen so that ideas are not summarily dismissed and can instead become real opportunities? The answer is a resounding YES!

Listening Fosters Innovation

In the *Fast Company* article "The 10 Faces of Innovation," the authors state that "Innovation is the lifeblood of organizations."[44] We will take that one step further and say that listening is fundamental to fostering innovation. For example, fully listening to someone share an idea for two minutes without interrupting them, focusing entirely on what they are saying and not trying to formulate your response, brings a deeper level of understanding—for you and for them. They will have the opportunity to expand on what they are thinking, and you will have a chance to listen for more clarity. Even honoring silence without trying to fill it can foster more productive communication. Innovation in the way you listen can even be a valuable tool in addressing societal issues, as the following story illustrates.

In Tanzania, girls faced a major barrier to finishing school and pursuing their futures, an obstacle that gave Florence another chance to shift her listening. As stated on the Amref. org/Tanzania: "Thousands of girls in Africa are at risk of FGM (Female Genital Mutilation), the harmful traditional practice of piercing or cutting a girl's genitalia to signify passage into womanhood. FGM often leads to child marriage and forced removal from school—putting a stop to girls' dreams."[45] Besides thwarting their ambitions, FGM involves massive pain and a lifetime of health problems, including complications in childbirth, which can lead to the mother's death.

Florence knew there needed to be an alternative. Nice Nailantei Leng'ete—one of *Time* magazine's 100 most influential people in the world in 2018—was a young pioneer in creating Alternative Rites of Passage (ARP) in the neighboring country of Kenya. After running away from home to avoid her own FGM at age eight, the teenager began verbally debating the males in her village and passionately asked them to end the practice.

Florence saw the value of the connection between the ARP and what her team was trying to accomplish. Their efforts expanded on the ARP program in Tanzania. With community leaders, AMREF teams spent three days with the girls educating them about topics such as sex education, HIV prevention, self-confidence, and human rights. Their parents were encouraged to not allow cutting and let the girls remain in school. Finally, the whole community celebrated. There was a proud procession of the girls who were dressed in their finest. The girls danced and sang. Keeping with Maasai tradition, the elders blessed the girls.

Trying to spread an alternative rite throughout a population of 59 million people on a community-by-community basis was going to take several lifetimes. Florence and her team needed another way. They decided to approach the Ministry of Health and Social Welfare. After several meetings, one of the deputy ministers agreed to attend an ARP in a community. He was treated as the guest of honor at the ceremony. Afterward, he said, "I want this to be rolled out across the country." It was not a quick victory, however. It took efforts to:

✦ Have another deputy observe the celebration.

✦ Solicit an investment by an aid funder from the Netherlands.

✦ Invite the deputy to an FGM forum that was held at the AMREF-led Africa Health Agenda International Conference.

✦ Foster extensive collaboration.

After three years, a national guideline was issued. This is a commendable milestone. However, in the battle for health and well-being, the challenges never stop. One new challenge is eliminating the stigma against marrying a woman who has not undergone FGM. Another is the ability to track girls who did not undergo FGM if they remain so until marriage and beyond.

Listening for Self

Dr. Temu demonstrated the ability to listen to and believe in yourself. When she returned from the California WLW program, she says she felt more confident. She let go of her self-doubt. She saw that she was underestimating herself. She listened to another voice inside saying, "I have the capacity; I will not hesitate." This fundamental shift allowed her to know that she could reach people—even senior officials in the government agencies. She added the leadership program to her curriculum vitae, and people started asking her about her global leadership experience.

We often are the least generous when we listen to our own internal dialogues—those voices in our heads. The voices can be positive or negative. Frequently, the voices are negative based on our filters. Some people postulate that if we spoke to others the way we speak to ourselves, we would not have any friends. Have you ever thought, "I can't do this"? When someone asks for a meeting with you (especially a superior), do you think, "What did I do wrong?" When the phone rings, do you ever think, "What do they want from me now?" When something bad happens, do you silently say, "How could I be so stupid?" All these thoughts, when acknowledged, are opportunities to recognize the influence of history and shift the context.

Other people's negative comments can fuel our internal conversations. When we accept them without questioning them, we can suffer substantial damage. Pat Obuchowski, the author of *Gutsy Women Win*, wrote:

> All during my life, I have encountered people who were naysayers and tried to belittle my ambitions. There was a time when I truly believed those who told me: "You can't do that!"; "That's too big for you to do"; Who do you think you are?"; and the proverbial "We've tried that before, and it won't work!" Well, I am a very different person today. I will listen to the naysayers and find the truth in what they say, but I no longer think what they say is the truth.[46]

When Pat stopped listening to the thoughts that came from others' automatic listening, she became more successful as an author.

"Keep away from people who try to belittle your ambitions. Small people always do that, but the really great make you feel that you, too, can become great."[47]

—MARK TWAIN

Shifting Listening

So, once we are aware of how we and others listen, how do we shift it? What do we shift it to? What new context can we create? How can we alter our impact on those around us?

In a workshop many years ago, my teacher Barbara Fittipaldi taught us to "listen for the gold in what others are saying." She went on to encourage us to *believe* that there is gold, not just think that there *might* be some. Another workshop suggested listening to find out what the other person cares about when they are speaking. If you have an organizational value such as fostering collaboration, you can be listening for any opportunity in what is being said for a chance to work together. If your organization is interested in growth, you can be listening for "How would this idea help us expand?"

The way you listen is important in other aspects of life besides work. One day, a friend noticed that she was tired of listening to her kids talk about the video games they were playing. She thought of those games as "stupid." Her impatience with them when they spoke about Grand Theft Auto or Mario Kart was so obvious that they sometimes avoided talking to her at all. They did not know that the source of her impatience was her listening with a predisposed judgment about the games. When she became aware of the situation, she shifted to listening for what they were learning by playing those games and why they enjoyed the experience so much.

Another friend discovered that when she asked her husband, "How was your day?" that she was not really interested in what he had to say. She shifted the question to "What was a highlight of your day?" She started listening for what was important to him as reflected in what he said.

In the end, it may all be about curiosity as stated in this quote by Roy T. Bennett in *The Light in the Heart*: "Listen with curiosity . . . The greatest problem with communication is we don't listen to understand. We listen to reply. When we listen with curiosity, we don't listen with the intent to reply. We listen for what's behind the words."[48] We can all use more listening that results in questions like:

+ Can you tell me more about that?

+ What does that mean to you or others on your team?

+ Can you give me another example so I can understand what you are saying?

Listening with an Open Heart

Opening and closing one's heart is a matter of being human. The "heart" opens to pleasant experiences—to love or generosity or beauty. It closes as a means of protection—to keep one from being hurt. How can the heart be used as a means of shifting your listening?

Take a deep breath. Think of a wonderful time in your life. Was it at a family celebration like a wedding or a religious holiday? Was it because of someone giving you a gift that overwhelmed you? What about the smell of cookies baking in the oven? Perchance, it is the sound of a child's laughter or the feel of a newborn baby in your arms for the first time. Do you remember when a butterfly landed on your hand, or a spectacular sunset lit up the sky?

Feel the energy of any or all those experiences coming from the heart. There is an openness and a warmth in the center of your chest. The next time, when anger or resentment flood your being, remember one of those experiences and feel your heart open with a new listening. Use that open heart to generate empathy the next time a friend is experiencing sadness or frustration. Listen solely to witness and feel what they are feeling.

Finally, listen to your heart for yourself. It has a wealth of courage and inspiration. It is where you can connect with the North Star that is guiding your life.

APPRECIATIVE INQUIRY QUESTIONS TO PONDER

▨ *Discover*

✓ What is my automatic way of listening? How is that affecting what happens around me?

▨ *Dream*

✓ What do I want to be happening around me? (At home, at school, at work, etc.)

▨ *Design*

✓ How will I adjust my listening to hear the essence of what is being said?

✓ How can I do as Bennett suggested and listen for what is behind the words?

▨ *Deliver*

✓ How will I know when I am listening that way?

CHAPTER 10

Tears of Joy

WHAT IS IT LIKE TO EMBARK on a journey to shift the context of one's life and step into a bigger arena? The story of Catherine Wanjohi of Kenya explores just such a shift. Catherine says that her life began in 2009 when she attended the Women Leaders for the World (WLW) program. She describes the experience as both painful and joyful. She remembers waking several nights to hear her roommate, Lynn Hightower, crying. Lynn remembers the same experience but in reverse. Were these tears of joy for a new beginning? Or were they tears of sadness for an ending to a life of playing small? The sessions challenged them, and the women challenged each other, with probing questions such as:

✦ "What is your vision?"

✦ "You are a woman with so much courage, commitment, values, and talent. Is your vision big enough given who you are?"

✦ "What brings you joy about that?"

Gradually, Catherine came to see that her organization, LifeBloom International, was more than a nongovernmental organization that taught vocational skills. It would be a place where vulnerable women would transform into leaders in their community. Catherine would be responsible for co-creating an entirely different outlook for their lives. The story that follows relates the many courageous actions she undertook to achieve her vision.

Building a Vocational School

Even before the global pandemic, Kenya experienced diminished incomes, unemployment, underemployment, and general discontent. According to the World Bank, "The proportion of Kenyans living on less than the international poverty line (US$1.90 per day in 2011 PPP*) has declined from 43.6% in 2005/06 to 35.6% in 2015/16."[49] Tourism is a major source of foreign cash flow. Of course, that revenue is endangered due to the global decline in travel.

Kenya has a young population with 70 percent under age thirty. Unemployment is particularly high among both young males and young females. According to the Borgen Project, "In Kenyan regions that experience high poverty rates and low levels of gender equality, as little as 19 percent of the girls in the region are enrolled in local primary schools. In others, as few as 1 in 15 girls are enrolled in primary school."[50] Kenyan girls marry early—many before age eighteen.

Given the dismal job prospects and therefore lack of opportunity, many women (especially HIV widows with

---

* Purchasing Power Parity (PPP) helps to compare the economic parity of two currencies through a market basket approach.

children to feed) turn to prostitution as a way of earning a living. This often eventually results in incarceration. LifeBloom focuses on this vulnerable group of women. Catherine's vision upon leaving the Women Leaders for the World (WLW) program was to build a vocational school that could train these women after their release. Today, Catherine says, "The building of the school facility was a metaphor for the women's transformations. Together we built the school—brick by brick. Together, we co-created our new lives. We became leaders in our own lives, not victims of circumstances."

Yes, Catherine "walked through the fire" with them. In 2010 and 2011, she experienced challenges in her marriage. At the end of her struggles, she had something in common with those vulnerable women: she was a single mother. LifeBloom lost its funding, and she was without an income, unable to pay the rent, and alone as the head of a household with three children. The loss of her spouse exposed her to ridicule, humiliation, and embarrassment.

She faced trying times and difficult decisions. Should she return the foster child she had just welcomed into her home? How could she feed all her children and pay her counseling certificate fees? Where would she find the strength to follow through on her commitment to the school?

Difficulties did not stop there. She found a paying position as chair of the local water board and rumors circulated that they had hired a "prostitute." Some of her friends abandoned her because they feared tarnishing their reputations. She felt torn between the person with a vision for transforming vulnerable women and the person who questioned if that was really who she was. But she kept going. Her faith in God was one of her foundations. She often found herself crying at the altar in her church. She never gave up and knew that God would not give up on her. She sought counseling for herself and her children.

She cherished the pictures of the other women from her California 2009 class, particularly the sight of them decked out in native garb at graduation with smiles on their faces. She was buoyed by stories from her LifeBloom beneficiaries. They would say to her:

+ "Catherine, my boy just graduated from school!"

+ "Catherine, I just learned . . ."

+ "Catherine, thank you for listening to me."

Her travails made her appreciate the world in which these women lived. She understood their normal way of life. And they responded to her because she did not judge them. She accepted them as they were.

In 2010, she published her first book, *A Walk at Midnight: Journeying with Abused Women and Girls Towards Inner Dignity & Wholeness*. She says that writing it all down was cathartic; it helped her shed the baggage. She shed tears for what was ending and imagined what it would be like when her vision became a reality. She became a role model for others. Her resilience became visible to the world. She helped others find their own inner strength and personal resilience. She learned to allow her emotions—sadness, anger, joy, or whatever she was feeling—to flow.

Starting in 2011, she raised money to buy the land she needed to enact her vision through Global Giving, a United

States organization that provides funding to those outside the country. She enlisted some of the women beneficiaries to be laborers. They dug the foundation. She bought a brick-making machine, and the women learned to use it. The walls started going up, slowly and in fits and starts as funding became available. Today, two classrooms stand in Naivasha. They are home to those who aspire to build new lives.

What ended? In 2009, when Catherine went to the leadership program, in fact, by the very act of applying for the program, her view of herself as a leader was changing. By attending a transformational leadership education program, she was stepping onto her learning edge. The tears she shed as she thought about her vision and what it would demand of her were tears of grief at the death of an old part of her identity.

In 2010 and 2011, more of the pillars of her identity were destroyed. She was no longer a wife. She was no longer a breadwinner. She was no longer viewed as an upstanding member of the community. Who was she? Who was she becoming?

The transition was a difficult one. She sought support from her religion and her professional counselors. Her sister helped her pay the rent. She learned about human beings in transition through the stories she heard from LifeBloom's beneficiaries. She rose above the name-calling and wrote two more books about her experiences: *Awakening the Giant in You and Those in Your Circles* and *Stepping Up and Stepping Out*. All three of her books are available on Amazon.

The person who rose from the fire like a phoenix is a woman who stands proud, a leader who is a role model for her community, and a mother who cherishes children—her biological two and three by adoption. Catherine's story illustrates life's journey from tears to joy.

Transitions Call for Resilience

In uncertain and challenging times like those experienced by Catherine, one must call upon their reserves of resilience. Resilience is one's inner strength when confronted with circumstances beyond our knowledge and experience. The global pandemic has created just such conditions for many people around the world. We have questions about what will emerge once the world is free of all the uncertainty. Examples of those type questions are:

✦ As a social activist, how can my cause become more relevant?

✦ What will work be like for businesses? Or classroom experiences for university students? Or fundraising events for nonprofit organizations?

✦ Can young leaders quickly gain the experience necessary to successfully take over companies as baby boomers retire?

✦ What new technologies are just over the horizon that will disrupt the way we live, work, protest, and play?

Many aspects of human interactions will be changed or need to change due to the pandemic. In 1991, William Bridges and Susan Mitchell published their now well-known article, "Leading Transition: A New Model for Change."[51] In that article, they described three stages of transition: 1) endings, 2) the neutral zone, and 3) new beginnings. Being able to understand the characteristics of each stage can help people to understand what is happening and make acceptance easier. Let's look at them now.

Stage 1: Endings

Innovation requires letting go of old ways and, sometimes, even letting go of identity. Though sometimes sad and frightening, this ending is necessary for change to occur. Endings often engender emotions like sadness, anger, fear, shock, and denial. For instance, a child is going off to college. The parent may experience sadness that an era wherein they could protect their child from harm is ending or they may fear that they are losing control. Viewed from the young person's perspective, they are leaving a loving haven. They may feel sadness at leaving everything they know behind, and they may be fearful of having to make their way alone.

During the global pandemic, a business or organization that relied on in-person events had to adapt to online technologies. Those wonderful moments when hundreds of people rose to give a speaker a standing ovation were no longer possible. In their stead were smaller gatherings that cost a fraction of the larger convention center events. There may be sadness at the loss of personal interaction and the fear of the financial impacts of lower revenues.

Climate change is causing migration to occur around the globe. One example is the Biloxi-Chitimacha-Choctaw tribe in Louisiana.[52] For decades, rising sea levels and salt water intrusion has created increasingly difficult living conditions.

Some people in the tribe left. Others stayed, hoping that nature would reverse course—denying the need for action.

We sense that something familiar is disappearing and that a "new normal" is somewhere beyond the horizon. We may be afraid of the unknown. At times like these, we need to rely on our resilience—our inner strength to face whatever is happening.

Stage 2: The Neutral Zone

The neutral zone is unfamiliar territory and can be an unsettling time. Backpedaling or rushing forward are two attempts to escape the discomfort. If a person or a team can take some time to experience the neutral zone, it is a potential time of creativity. For example, with their child off at college, a parent may find they have more freedom to spend on activities they enjoyed before kids or maybe they will take up a new pastime. The college student may, at first, be reluctant to participate fully in campus life. This is a period of exploration to find new friends. It is time to experiment with different sports, foods, hairstyles, etc. With regard to the global pandemic, organizations found themselves going through a period of exploration:

+ What is the format for an outstanding online event?

+ What will people pay for shorter, more impersonal experiences?

+ How often should they be offered? Who are excellent speakers in this media?

And what of the Biloxi-Chitimacha-Choctaw tribe? The tribal elders began to formulate a plan to resettle the entire village. They applied to the U.S. Department of Housing and Urban Development (HUD) for a grant. In 2016, when they received $48 million, they began executing their plan.

During this stage, the future is becoming clearer, but there are still many unknowns to be faced. Resilience is required as progress is made, and setbacks occur. It takes real inner strength to remain in the neutral zone—not reverting to the past and not rushing into the future.

Stage 3: New Beginnings

Different behaviors and new routines involved in a new beginning may feel awkward at first. New habits and patterns are beginning to be established. This stage requires continual practice and, eventually, mastery. The parents adapt to their "empty nest" and enjoy the peace and quiet. The college student learns to balance studying and social events. The event company emerges as a leader in the domain of online seminars. Speakers seek them out as *the* "place" to be seen and heard. The tribe purchases new land and starts construction of homes.

The need for resilience is not over as this phase starts. Many challenges come with each step forward. It would be easy to slip back. Courage and steadfastness are required.

APPRECIATIVE INQUIRY QUESTIONS TO PONDER

Discover

✓ What is a transition you are in right now? Describe it in terms of the three stages just discussed.

Dream

✓ What do you want the "new beginning" of this transition to be?

Design

✓ What sources do you have to provide support for your transition? Think of people, spiritual touchstones, funding organizations, and the numerous resources that exist.

Deliver

✓ Take a step toward that new beginning today!

CHAPTER 11

Pausing Creates Innovation

ASHLIE BRYANT IS CEO AND COFOUNDER of 3Strands Global Foundation. This Sacramento-based nonprofit has a vision of a "world free from human trafficking." Their focus is on prevention education and reintegration. They have designed and implemented holistic approaches to help victims build new lives.

Human trafficking, despite what many people believe, does not just occur in other countries. It is a fast-growing and heinous crime in the United States. While the numbers are known to be underreported, there were an estimated 100,000 victims of human trafficking in the United States (Federal Bureau of Investigation, 2016).[53]

Guardian Group, a U.S.-based research organization, makes this point more poignantly: "Unlike other statistics you have come across in your life, the following statistics have a pulse; they are America's daughters, sisters, nieces and sometimes America's sons as well."[54] Human traffickers seek the most vulnerable youth—children in the child welfare system, those in the juvenile justice system, runaways, the homeless, etc. The average female who is trafficked is fifteen years old. The males are even younger.

Social media relationships are facilitating the building of trust with traffickers. The vulnerable youths want to belong and be loved. They think that the traffickers are offering those feelings. Sometimes traffickers take youths off the streets using coercion and fraud. Internet ads and custom sites facilitate the selling of "special" services. Eventually, locks on the doors become unnecessary. The victims remain with traffickers out of fear, isolation, guilt, shame, and misplaced loyalty.

It Can Happen Anywhere

Ashlie Bryant got involved in human trafficking activism after a close personal experience. Her friend's teenage daughter, at seventeen years old, caught a ride home from a local grocery store parking lot with her friends. They had been befriended by a twenty-two-year-old stranger, who they did not know was a human trafficker. Perpetrators create relationships and look for someone who is vulnerable. Unfortunately, after hours of hanging out with the teens, Ashlie's friend's daughter was the one that the trafficker picked as most vulnerable. She was taken to the trafficker's home and then sold online to another human trafficker who lived in another part of California. She was transported there, kept drugged and sold approximately fifteen to twenty times each day to men who were seeking to have sex with minors. The community mobilized and, with assistance from law enforcement, the girl was found and returned home after about eighteen days. Ashlie witnessed firsthand the devastating effects and trauma of this experience on her friend's daughter. Thus began her journey as cofounder of 3Strands Global Foundation.

In 2017, Ashlie attended the Women Leaders for the World program. She vividly remembers the part of the course relating to listening and questioning. She feels that listening to others was already one of her gifts. What the new material brought out in her was adding a pause and asking more questions to gain more information. She learned to resist the temptation to be formulating her own answer instead of truly hearing what the other person was saying. She found that she could be grounded and centered instead of rushing to "fix" whatever the other person said.

Settling an Argument

Ashlie describes a situation that arose when she returned to work from the WLW program. Two staff members were fighting and disrupting the rest of the staff. Having survived cancer a few years prior, Ashlie had no tolerance for fighting. She saw no reason for such behavior, especially in a nonprofit where everyone believes so strongly and passionately about the work.

She listened patiently to the two sides of the story. She trusted herself and her intuition. She told the two staff members that she had listened carefully to what they had said and had decided that they would need to make amends themselves or go their separate ways from the organization. While she knew both were important to the organization, she felt this ultimatum was the right way to put the responsibility on them to resolve their differences.

Upon further reflection, Ashlie realized that she tended to be the "fixer" in 3Strands. What do people bring to the attention of a "fixer"? They bring her problems. Ashlie's ingrained characteristics of being a good listener and encouraging others was, in fact, limiting her leadership. There was a vicious cycle of see a problem, fix a problem, see another problem, fix another problem. It is easy for this cycle to arise, particularly in the nonprofit world where it is all about fixing ingrained societal problems.

Creating a Vacuum

Ashlie is committed to her vision—ending slavery. She also knows that being too emotionally attached caused her, in moments of stress, to be off-center and hurried. In conversations where she practiced listening openly and pausing, she found herself in a calm place to foster well-thought-out decisions. That calmness created a vacuum at 3Strands, which was filled with innovation. Imagine that! A shift in the pace and quality of conversations drew out more innovative ideas from those around her.

Ashlie noticed another consequence of her improved listening skills. She saw that it helped her think more clearly with those who tend to see the world as black or white. Young staff members do not yet know how to see the subtle shades of gray that surround many issues at a nonprofit. Some even seem to see the world through a lens of "You are either with me or against me." When Ashlie models pausing to think and insists on others using the same technique, there is less defensiveness.

The flip side of listening is the ability of a leader to ask questions to shift the context of a conversation. Ashlie recalls one conversation with her lawyer over licensing rights. He had found what he viewed was a violation of their contract for materials to teach young people how to identify possible trafficking situations.

As the conversation unfolded, Ashlie could see that he had a whole rift of assumptions. It is a natural pattern to make assumptions and jump to a conclusion. She started asking him questions that drew another picture, that brought another possible scenario into existence. He began to see that there were, in fact, potential circumstances under which this was not an attempt to circumvent their contract. The conversation ended with a promise to review the situation in more detail, including the broader context. The role of great questions is to help examine the underlying assumptions.

Inviting New Futures

Ashlie's listening is uncovering new opportunities for 3Strands. A recent meeting with a large company that serves 25 percent of the foster families in the country illustrates this. Ashlie started the meeting by presenting the facts about how the U.S. social welfare system is broken. She talked about her organization's results in preventing trafficking and stopping exploitation. As she listened carefully to their questions, she realized that they were talking about wider concepts of empowerment, resilience, and connectedness with foster families. With this understanding of how they wanted to serve their clients, she began to reframe the partnership. She had envisioned a more limited path. Now she saw new ways to reach 100,000 foster youths—to empower a generation. Alignment was possible when she really understood their vision for the future and could recast how 3Strands could play into that opportunity.

What Is Possible Given Dedication?

Ashlie Bryant has led 3Strands Global to many accomplishments in the years since its founding. The California Assembly Bill No. 1227 was championed by 3Strands through the legislative process and signed by Governor Jerry Brown. School districts in that state must ensure that all pupils in grades seven to twelve are informed (at an age-appropriate level) about sexual harassment, sexual assault, adolescent relationship abuse, intimate partner violence, and human trafficking.

In 2018, 3Strands and their partners launched their PROTECT (prevention) program. As of 2021, it has been adopted in six states and soon a few other countries. In 2020, the federal government announced a grant program for eight local education agencies across the nation. 3Strand's PROTECT program is a subrecipient in four locations.

Because trafficking is more than prevention and protection, 3Strands has expanded their program of placing trafficked individuals in sustainable, trauma-informed jobs with employers who understand their unique needs. Through their Employ + Empower program, they have been able to find employment for more than 350 individuals.

Leadership from Within

Ashlie says that she once viewed leadership as a series of things that people do. She now believes in the concept of leadership from within. She says that she is more of a leader because of embracing that idea. She has taken on leadership roles outside her organization at the state and national level. With the Biden administration, she believes this is the time when there can be widespread progress to take care of children. She is working to create a "child welfare collaboration" where people from many points of view come together and listen with pauses for thinking. That is where innovation and change will happen.

APPRECIATIVE INQUIRY QUESTIONS TO PONDER

▪ *Discover*

✓ What are your ingrained characteristics of being a listener? In what ways are these habits limiting your growth as a leader?

✓ In your life, where are you identified as being a fixer? What is the effect on your leadership?

✓ In your leadership, discover a place where it is appropriate to take action to shift the context.

▪ *Dream*

✓ What would it be like if there were more innovative discussions at work? At home?

▪ *Design*

✓ How will you design a new future for yourself or organization by listening and asking different questions to shift the context?

▪ *Deliver*

✓ In what ways will you sustain your dream to fulfill your vision of how to listen?

PART FOUR

Embodying Leadership

CHAPTER 12

Giving My Own Dream Priority

DITI MOOKHERJEE COMES FROM A WELL-TO-DO Indian family. In 2010, she became a Fulbright-Nehru scholar at Santa Clara University working with the environmental studies department. During the last months of her assignment, she heard about the Women Leaders for the World program and applied. That was her first step toward becoming the leader of a youth movement.

From the day she stepped into the seminar, she was on a journey to becoming a different person—one who is using her life's energy in new ways. Being raised as a woman in the Indian culture, Diti focused her early life on making others happy, supporting their visions, and being a good daughter, wife, and mother. Her father and husband encouraged her to be free, but social norms made sure that she was not totally independent, either. She was trained to listen for what others wanted, not to what she desired.

In a profound moment during the WLW seminar in 2011, she gave her own dream priority. She recalls that it was dark outside. (Sunset comes early in December in Northern California.) She heard the workshop leader saying, "Let go of the person who came here. What do *you* connect with? What is *your* vision?" She chose to put herself first—to trust herself with a ferocity she had never used for her own ideas. She would work with youth and nature. She embraced her calling—something she could not ignore.

Embracing Her Own Dream

Diti became the leader who promoted "Youth nurtures nature; Nature nurtures peace." She called the young people she worked with Green Rhinos. She spoke her dream of creating 10,000 of them. She would bring them together to discover their own dreams and to launch small scale projects to positively impact nature in their localities.

Today, Diti is on her way to that goal as CEO of Association for Social and Environmental Development. More than 5,000 youths have participated in projects such as planting thousands of trees in the delta along the Ganges, Brahmaputra, and Meghna Rivers in the Sundarbans. Along the way, amazing and unexpected transformations have occurred.

Green Rhinos are more confident. They trust themselves and their own vision of a better world. They feel the fire and power that is generated when they are working *together* toward a project that makes a difference. They have learned about collaboration by jointly digging holes for the plants. They enjoy being on teams instead of fiercely competing for individual recognition at school. They are entrepreneurial spirits who have overcome the fears of asking their principals and others in the community for support.

Each time Diti meets with the youths, she feels joy. She

knows that she is in the right place. She teaches and, in fact, embodies three principles:

1. There is no wrong vision; because it is yours, it is real and legitimate.

2. Everyone has a right to speak and has something to contribute.

3. When someone speaks to us, we listen.

The youths, mostly middle schoolers, are like sponges. They not only hear her words, but they also see that she lives them. She has become her three principles.

It Is No Use Going Back to Yesterday

Was it a smooth road from that California seminar to where Diti is today? No, far from it.

Diti says it was difficult to go back to the same situation she had left. She was not the same person who departed for California. Yes, her husband was there to support her, but he felt that there had been a significant shift. At first, he found it hard to understand her. One of her best friends admitted, "I am afraid to talk to her now." Like Alice in Wonderland, however, she knew "It's no use going back to yesterday; I was a different person then."

Feelings of being lost and alone engulfed her. It was like she had nothing to hold on to in the world. She sought like-minded people. She searched for funding. She pursued every opportunity that presented itself. She launched a partnership with an organization that was giving solar lamps to youths in the Sundarbans. To get a lamp, they had to attend Diti's seminar. Both physical and psychological light was brought into the young people's lives.

At times she was filled with self-doubt. She tried to be patient. Her classical Indian music practice and yoga sustained and restored her. She says, "When my thoughts get stuck and my energy wanes, music and yoga help me to regain my equilibrium. I can then attain and maintain the 'sweet space' of quiet and peace. Into that space, energy and excitement move freely. I am ready to be myself again."

Some brilliant people came to help her. Her workshop leader, Barbara Fittipaldi, was a constant advisor. She had the support of others from her class who were going through the same experience.

A Life of Its Own

Diti gradually came to enjoy what she was doing, to be less serious, to play with the project. Soon, less effort was needed. With this ease came insights. She clearly saw what the program was creating in the students. She comprehended that this was not *her* program anymore. It now belonged to the Green Rhinos themselves. It had developed a life of its own. Diti let go of ownership. She says, "It is my sacred duty to be able to remain a channel for it and not let it get stuck."

Diti plans to expand her focus on "Nature nurtures peace." She ran a successful project in which nineteen Indian schools and ten American schools studied water. There was local voting on whose projects were best. One team from India visited Kentucky, and another from the United States visited Kolkata. In Kolkata, the team from Kentucky shared their stories and proudly showed off their United States project. The Indian youths did the same during their American tour. With more exchanges like this, Diti believes peace will emerge. The young people will know each other as real people who are connected through a common bond of understanding and nurturing nature.

So why is this a story of embodiment? Diti's embodiment of her vision is never more evident than when she coaxes the children to speak about their own visions. She is a quiet spirit who is helping them find the passion within themselves. She uses her musical practice and spirituality to remain centered and congruent with her deep caring. Her actions, her words, and even her body motions are melded together, revealing her openness in an inviting way. When she speaks, she uses the youths' own words—reflecting how carefully she listens and connects to them. She acknowledges each contribution as valuable.

APPRECIATIVE INQUIRY QUESTIONS TO PONDER

Discover

✓ What leadership values and principles are you embodying?

Dream

✓ What is a personal dream you have where you can put yourself first?

✓ Let yourself go and dream about embracing this personal dream!

Design

✓ What has to change to make this dream a priority in your life?

Deliver

✓ Outline two to three steps you can take now towards that priority.

CHAPTER 13

100 Million People
Part of the Economy

SOUTH AFRICA IS A COUNTRY of 60 million people. Politically, it is infamous as the home of *apartheid* from 1948 until the late 1980s. This was a system of institutionalized *racial segregation that fostered not only inequality in human rights but also in economic conditions.* This resulted in almost 50 percent of the adult population living in poverty.

The lowest of South African poverty lines—the food poverty line—is defined as someone living without the ability to purchase the nutritional equivalent of 2,100 calories per day—a minimum established by the United Nations. This means they are living on less than about $40 per month. Twenty-five percent of South Africans fall below this minimal bar. These numbers have grown during the global pandemic.

Financial inclusion is needed in South Africa. Most of those living below the poverty line are unbanked and underserved by financial institutions. While small loans to start microenterprises are required to spark the economy, the lack of financial history prohibits creating normal credit scores for previously marginalized individuals.

Priya Thakoor and Philile Mkhize are two young women

professionals from South Africa. They came together for Women Leaders for the World in 2017. They were the cofounders of a financial enterprise called CommuScore. Their dream was to create an alternate credit score for the many unbanked South Africans by using information from a network of savings groups that operate like village banks.

Financial Freedom for Everyone

Philile expressed her dream while in WLW with a four-word stimulating statement: "Financial Freedom for Everyone." At that time, she was working on an alternate means of credit identity. She and Priya were developing technology that would collect and analyze information from village banks. They would report on those who were saving even small amounts on a regular basis. This would encourage people to trust the financial institutions and to demonstrate their commitment to savings groups. Based on this demonstration, a rating system could be implemented, and information provided back to the banks for loan consideration. The pandemic brought economic hardship to Priya and Philile, so they abandoned the credit score project for now to return to being employees in the financial sector.

Priya and Philile became employed by large financial institutions. They now hold the same dream in a different form. They dream that 100 million people will be part of the economy through not only a credit score system but also productive jobs that provide a living wage.

Priya and Philile both say that their stimulating statements created at WLW are embodied deeply inside them. Their value of empathy led them to look for new organizations that were founded on people-type principles when CommuScore had to be put on hold. They say that they feel more grounded during stressful times and respect everyone's perspective—their human perspectives. They are both seen in their organizations as leaders with highly tuned listening skills.

They say that the global pandemic has created a greater need for putting humans first. When offices were closed due to the lockdown, many workers did not have access to computers in their homes. They would not be able to continue working and receiving a salary if they did not have this vital tool. People stepped forward who were willing to volunteer to take computers to their coworkers. Because it is difficult to find locations in the suburbs as well as the fact that they can be dangerous places when carrying expensive equipment, the volunteers put their own health and safety at risk for their friends.

Embodiment in the Workplace

Priya and Philile knew when they formed CommuScore that they cared about financial freedom. Their startup was an expression of that care. As they were forced to abandon their dream, the form of that care changed; it was now more universal. They carried their care for financial freedom to their new organizations. Others in those organizations recognized that they were centered and passionate about equality.

Like Priya and Philile, to maximize our leadership impact, we must make our bodies, thoughts, words, and deeds congruent. Our bodies are magnificent instruments that, when fully and properly used, impart meaning to our actions. As leaders, how do we demonstrate the following:

✦ Respecting others

✦ Seeking justice

✦ Being grateful

✦ Caring for the environment

We listen carefully to others' ideas and support putting them into action. We take stands for human rights and give to charities that are forwarding them. We express appreciation to our colleagues by organizing recognition events. We conserve electricity and water every day.

As embodied leaders, we come from a place of wholeness. By using techniques such as deep breathing, we allow distractions or negative emotions to flow away. Our bodies are more attuned to our feelings. When we speak from our hearts, our voice has power because it is based in authenticity. We can come from the present and be fully with others, making it easier for them to connect with us. An important part of embodiment is how it is perceived by others.

To be successful, today's organizations need leaders who embody the qualities that are essential to thrive in the new environment—openness, creativity, and boldness, to name just a few. Imagine a team where everyone embodies their most important values. What could they accomplish?

Are opportunities to be leaders only present in organizations outside our home? Or are we leaders in our families and of ourselves? If we are not a person with a title, are there opportunities to lead? Is everyone in an organization a leader? If we care about having a loving relationship with our partner, how can we embody love? If we want to be a loving grandparent for many years, how can we embody the ability to stay healthy? If we want to reverse climate change, what can we do personally and what can we do to support clean energy? If we believe that diversity leads to innovation, how can we bring more people who are different from us into our organization?

Appreciative Inquiry Questions to Ponder

▧ *Discover*

✓ What action have you taken that came from your embodying what you care about?

▧ *Dream*

✓ List five new ways that you embrace what you care about. Pay attention to different domains of your life—for example, family, health, spirituality, organization, and community.

▧ *Design*

✓ Craft a commitment to one of these new ways—for example, "I am a committed to maintaining the natural state of our coastline."

▧ *Deliver*

✓ Plan an activity for the next week that demonstrates that you are embodying your commitment. For example, "I will volunteer three hours next week to clean up the beach."

CHAPTER 14

She Can Speak from Her Heart

Lucky Chhetri is the founder and a director of Three Sisters Adventure Trekking, an "organization for women and by women." They are demonstrating that women are as physically and mentally as strong as men. Lucky also cofounded and helps operate Empowering Women of Nepal (EWN), a nonprofit that provides training and other benefits for the villages along the trekking routes.

Nepal is a spectacularly beautiful country that lies near the "top of the world." The Himalaya mountains dominate its geography. Tourism is one of the fastest-growing industries. Prior to the 2020 lockdowns from the pandemic, it contributed about 8 percent to the country's GDP. The Annapurna trekking circuit is one of its many tourist attractions.

Even with a robust tourist trade, Nepal is one of the poorest countries in the world. It suffers from a lack of natural resources, challenging terrain, and ineffective government. Unemployment and underemployment are estimated to affect almost half of the population.

Before Lucky and her sisters, Dicky and Nicky, began to train women as guides, all treks in Nepal were led by males.

The sisters saw an opportunity to provide female guides, especially for female guests who were traveling alone and wanted assurance of their safety from sexual harassment along the trails. They had to break through many cultural and physical barriers. Their philosophy of "when we emerge from fear, we can do great things" helped them through those first days.

Over the last twenty-five years, Three Sisters Trekking has received many awards for helping stimulate the economy of their country and for their impact on women. They proudly state that their goal is to "encourage our sisters to become self-supportive, independent, decision-making women."

Speaking From Her Heart

In 2007, a prior graduate recommended to Lucky that she attend the Women Leaders for the World program. Lucky recalls that she and other participants cried a lot. She says, "We were cleansing ourselves and coming out of our boxes. The program had us discussing who we were being, and crying was our way of letting go of the limitations and fears we had discovered." Metaphorically, "coming out of our boxes" meant opening up to new possibilities and discovering the person we were becoming. Lucky shares that, during this process, she felt supported by the faculty and staff with "so many powerful women sharing and nurturing us."

Lucky noticed a difference in herself when she returned to Nepal. She became a self-confident public speaker and was invited to speak in different settings around the world. Her confidence surprised her because she did not receive any specific instruction on public speaking. Lucky realized that her ability to speak confidently came from knowing who she is and from speaking from her heart. She embodied her vision of women trekking safely not only in the Himalayas but in their respective personal lives throughout Nepal.

Lucky attributes many of her accomplishments to her regular meditation practice, which creates feelings of calmness and centeredness. As the Nepal tourism industry collapsed, Lucky retained an optimistic outlook. Resilience is a natural part of her Nepalese culture. She and others accept that everything is temporary. Even in the pandemic, she sees a silver lining. She is taking the time to rest, celebrate, and enjoy family togetherness. Her attitude is that "every challenge teaches me something." Lucky even saw this as a time to know herself better. Her attitude is a reminder of the Rumi quote, "Why should I be unhappy? Every parcel of my being is in full bloom."

APPRECIATIVE INQUIRY QUESTIONS TO PONDER

▦ *Discover*

✓ What are some of the physical and cultural barriers you have broken through in your life and career? How has it felt as you stepped through to the other side? What are some you still want to surmount?

▦ *Dream*

✓ What is your dream for speaking from your heart to the world and sharing what you deeply care about?

▦ *Design*

✓ Fashion a few sentences that genuinely represent your deepest care.

▦ *Deliver*

✓ What regular practices will you incorporate into your life to sustain you during challenging times?

CHAPTER 15

They Lose the Frightened Look in Their Eyes

Phionah Musumba is no stranger to fear and personal loss. As a teenage mother, she watched her child die in her arms because she could not afford medical assistance. Since then, she has become a crusader to prevent other girls' suffering. When she attended a Women Leaders for the World (WLW) program in 2017, her vision was to build a girls' STEM (Science, Technology, Engineering & Math) school. During the global pandemic, she pivoted her organization, Malkia Foundation, to provide hope and support to the growing wave of unwanted pregnant teenage girls.

According to the World Bank, "Globally, 35 percent of women have experienced physical and/or sexual intimate partner violence, or sexual violence by a non-partner."[55] Unfortunately, in 2020, according to the website Unwomen.org, "Calls to helplines have increased five-fold in some countries as rates of reported intimate partner violence increase because of the COVID-19 pandemic. Restricted movement, social isolation, and economic insecurity are increasing women's vulnerability to violence in the home around the world."[56]

Phionah witnessed the increase in teen pregnancies

firsthand as local primary and secondary schools were closed in Kenya. The ensuing lockdown in small home spaces escalated violence against women and girls. In too many cases, victims of sexual violence became pregnant. This initiates a plunge into what Barbara Brown Taylor, author of *Learning to Walk in the Dark,* calls a "dark" period.

Naturally, the darkness of sexual violence is filled with emotions. There may be fear of being assaulted again. Fear that one has lost control of their lives. There may be guilt, shame, and embarrassment. Often, victims wonder, "How was I to blame for this?" Sadness is common and may develop into depression. There is hopelessness and despair—even thoughts of suicide.

The discovery of pregnancy only deepens the uncertainties of the darkness. *How am I going to take care of myself while pregnant? What is happening to my body? Why am I moody, sad, tired, etc.? How will I care for the child after it is born? Will I ever be able to return to school and have a normal life?* Pregnant teens have real fears of dying in childbirth. While most of the developed world experiences from two to ten deaths per 100,000 births, many African countries average between 500 and 1,200.[57]

Unmarried pregnant adolescents everywhere in the world face rejection by friends and family. Phionah sees some thrown out of their homes—shunned by their families who are ashamed or feeling guilty. Most of these girls have never had more than the equivalent of $1 in their pockets. They have not been financially responsible for themselves, let alone for the prospect of having to provide for and care for a newborn.

Lighting the Dark

PHIONAH SEES THEIR SUFFERING AS A chance to bring some light into their lives and to change their outlook on how life will be. Malkia Foundation training takes place over a seven-week period. They provide training in financial literacy, handling money, and starting a microbusiness.

When pregnant mothers graduate, they receive a loan of approximately $30 to start their microbusiness. Many become street vendors—offering potato fries, fruit, and/or vegetables by the roadsides. Phionah says they show "amazing commitment" with over 85 percent eventually repaying their loans. Some are reentering school and paying their fees out of their own pockets. She also sees them "lose the look of fear in their eyes."

Inner Strength

Where has Phionah found the courage and resilience to bring light into her own family and to create it in the community? She modestly says that she has "never known I was strong." She remembers her nineteen-year-old daughter once telling her that, "Momma, I have never seen a woman as strong as you." Her strength comes from embodying her commitment to making life better for those around her, especially through education. She believes that education "enlightens you in so many ways."

She credits an increase in self-confidence after WLW with her ability to do public speaking about the many issues facing African women leaders. She has even been asked to talk about empowerment to members of her high school class. She was shocked by a request from them to speak because her peers had treated her as useless. As she talked to them about her journey, she stood tall and proud. She embodied her commitment to make her own and others' lives better, despite the circumstances. What brought her to action was, in fact, her fear. She was terrified that her daughters would live in poverty and fear as she herself had for so many years.

Phionah points to a turning point in her life. In 2014, she applied for the Community Solutions Program.[58] When accepted, she met people from different walks of life and exchanged ideas and experiences. She built herself up to go beyond.

When she started Disadvantaged Girls (the root of Malkia Foundation), she was a city dweller. The work was supported by funds from her own pocket made at odd jobs. She decided to go back to her rural home. Here she found that her ideas were labeled as "Phionah's foreign ideas." She was teaching the use of sanitary towels—far more hygienic than the banana fibers and sand used by other women. She was even arrested for doing that work. Fortunately, recommendation letters from a Nairobi nongovernmental organization got her out of custody.

From these humble beginnings, Malkia Foundation has arisen. It has received a $95,000 grant to fund basic operations for six years. Land has been purchased to build the STEM school for girls. Phionah's hope is that will be finished for a 2022 class.

Darkness and Light for Leaders

We all experience dark and light periods in our lives. When we are plunged into family crisis, health emergencies, losing a job, or our organizations are in turmoil, we are filled with anxiety and doubt. We fear what we do not understand and what we cannot control. We believe that we "should" know how to get out. It is important to understand that dark periods are just as much learning experiences as our days in the light. If we can quiet the judgments that occur because we think that something should not be happening, we can better stay centered and project calmness to others.

APPRECIATIVE INQUIRY QUESTIONS TO PONDER

▦ *Discover*

✓ Think about a "dark" time in your life and identify the lessons you took away from it.

▦ *Dream*

✓ Draw an image of yourself living without judgment in a future dark period. This may look like a brain surrounded by darkness with a question mark inside it or whatever you can think of.

▦ *Design*

✓ Identify one way you can bring a sense of calm into your life.

▦ *Deliver*

✓ Do this calming practice every day for the next week first thing in the morning.

PART FIVE

Empowering Interpretations

CHAPTER 16

It Is Not *Charity*

WE INTRODUCED YOU TO ALMA COTA DE YANEZ in Chapter 6. Today, Alma's organization, FESAC, generates and coordinates donations of money and time for almost forty nongovernmental organizations (NGOs), serving 50,000 people. Their activities encompass the fields of health, education, the environment, violence against women, and many more social issues. Under Alma's leadership, FESAC annually mobilizes almost $1 million for these causes.

How did Alma jump from leading a network of ten NGOs with ten computers to becoming a major force for good in just fifteen years? She built on her newfound capacity to create networks and learned to reframe through language.

What do you think of when you hear the word *charity*? Do you see a homeless person in the street holding out their hand? Do you think about the local food bank or soup kitchen? How different is your image when you hear the words *social investment*? Do you imagine people gaining skills to support themselves? Is this an effort "to achieve a combination of economic and social and/or environmental goals"? This transformation in language from *charity* to *social investment* fueled Alma and FESAC's move into being a major forces in Nogales.

Creating Social Investment as a Driving Force

By changing from "giving to charity" to "encouraging social investment," Alma could enlist government officials, business-men and women, academics, and ordinary citizens across the border in Tucson and in Green Valley, Arizona. City officials wanted a "cleaner, healthier, and safer" city that could attract American tourists with money to spend. People begging for a handout outside the restaurants did not enhance people's appetites. *Maquiladora* (the twin plant) managers wanted workers who did not miss work because their children were sick. Universities wanted internships where their students could fulfill their 480 hours of required social service and gain real experience. Retired doctors and dentists wanted a way to continue to use their skills and help the many who could not afford medical care across the border.

As the provider of opportunities for social investment, Alma thrives on the broad scope of her FESAC activities. She says, "My job provides contact on a regular basis with people who have millions of dollars in their accounts and others, like just deported migrants, who own only what they are wearing." She has learned to use humor, "an asset in this job," to appeal for donations. "My donors are usually men, very rich and very Catholic, so going to heaven matters to them. I make it clear that supporting us might help a little."

So, Alma became a networker extraordinaire, and FESAC became the hub of social investment activity in Nogales. She created a menu of projects that would improve the city where they lived and worked. Perhaps the star on that list is ARSOBO—the Arizona Sonora Border

Organization—launching inclusion projects. Their factory supplies all-terrain wheelchairs, hearing aids, and prosthetics for those who cannot afford them at "retail" prices. ARSOBO employs people with disabilities as their factory workers. So, they are a ray of hope in a field of hopelessness.

The FESAC website discusses "social investment" as follows:

> Generosity is one of the noblest values of the human being and helping other people is undoubtedly one of the most rewarding things in our life.
>
> FESAC understands and lives the value of acting selflessly in favor of those who need it most and invites all those institutions and people committed to their community to make their donations and thus improve the quality of life of many Sonoran residents.
>
> We promote social investment as a social responsibility strategy through sustainable projects and/or programs that meet the interests of social investors, promoting community development with the aim of achieving greater social cohesion and participation.

The ARSOBO website tells the story of a typical aid recipient—a fisherman named Francisco. He was an enterprising fisherman until he lost his leg in a car accident. While he had barely scraped by in the best of times, now his family was desperate. Since males are supposed to provide for their wife and children, he felt "less like a man." A prothesis from normal sources cost $2,000—a price he could not afford.

ARSOBO charges $500 to those disadvantaged people who, like Francisco, cannot afford them from other sources.

Besides prosthetics, they supply hearing aids and several different wheelchairs—all at affordable prices to poorer Mexicans.

How is this possible? It is possible because numerous partners make "social investments." The factory that houses ARSOBO was donated. The paint on the walls is that "wrong color" you return to Home Depot. The returned paint cans pile up in the store's back room until they are retrieved to serve social investment. The sound chamber that tests auditory abilities is secondhand; it is from the University of Arizona. Money for materials comes from donations made through the Border Community Alliance (BCA), a Green Valley, USA, organization. Restaurants such as the local La Roca support the enterprise. Numerous individuals donate their time and skills to train workers, improve product quality, and keep operations going.

Enterprises like ARSOBO are possible in Nogales because Alma transformed the stigma of charity (of "handouts") into a possibility named "social investment."

Learning more positive ways to verbalize initiatives and decisions is fundamental to leadership. When we respond to a problem at work or at home by asking, "What happened? Who did it? How did this ever occur?" we build an environment of mistrust. If, instead, we encourage looking at the bigger picture and ask, "What worked? What did not work? What was missing from the situation?" we foster a calmer, more analytic culture. If we can examine each situation as a learning experience—a place to create from—we can ask, "What is possible now?" and thus advance a generative outlook.

APPRECIATIVE INQUIRY QUESTIONS TO PONDER

Discover

✓ What words do you currently use to describe something you want to shift? (In other words, how are you currently framing a problem?)

Dream

✓ Describe what the future would look like if that problem disappeared.

Design

✓ What is a short phrase that describes that utopian state? (The best ones paint a picture for the listener. For example, "Placing books in the hands of every child—dropping seeds on well-watered soil.")

Deliver

✓ Write an email to someone asking for their assistance using your new language.

CHAPTER 17

Could You Make That YOUR Own Initiative?

FROM 2000 UNTIL 2018, TURKEY MADE steady progress in building its economy. Turkey's GDP is $760 billion USD as of 2020—earning a ranking of twentieth in the world. The GDP per capita is approximately $9,000 USD. This masks, however, extreme income disparity between the large metropolitan areas such as Istanbul, Ankara, and Izmir and rural areas. There are also gender inequalities with less than one-third of adult women in the labor force. Women also earn 40 percent less on average than men.[59]

Sema Basol is a woman from Turkey who has lived in the United States for many years. Sema attended Boğaziçi University in Istanbul for her undergraduate education and then came to the United States to get her Master of Business Administration at the University of California, Los Angeles. She went to work at Mattel, home of the Barbie doll and other successful children's toys. At Mattel Inc., as director of consumer products, she built Mattel brands into new businesses that generated annual retail sales of over half billion dollars in international markets. Being a "superwoman," she also was raising two children.

Fast-forward to the early part of the twenty-first century. Sema and her husband, Bulent, were empty nesters who split their time between San Jose and Manhattan Beach, California. Bulent was involved with an energy startup, and Sema was searching for what would be next in her career and life. It was at this point that she became a volunteer with the Global Women's Leadership Network (GWLN) and its Women Leaders for the World (WLW) program.

Sema fell in love with the leadership program and wanted to take it to Turkey. During a 2017 trip home, she convinced me (Linda), the executive director of GWLN, to join her in Istanbul to look for potential partners. The trip was a success; two influential Turkish women would attend the summer program in California.

While volunteering with the program that year, Sema (and the two Turkish attendees) birthed a dream for Turkish women. Why not physically take the program to Istanbul? Sema had learned to enroll others in her vision, so soon, funds were raised, airline tickets purchased, and attendees invited. Sema was committed and speaking her vision broadly. Then, almost as quickly as it had appeared, the opportunity evaporated. A major roadblock appeared: a change in the priorities of one key partner led to cancellation of the entire project. Sema was surprised and disappointed. In her own eyes and those of others involved in the project, she was a failure.

Sema's Turkish conservative business philosophy did not match the mentality of Silicon Valley. It is one of the few places in the world where "failing fast" is prized. By failing fast, California entrepreneurs mean that they push the development of their products because there is no replacement for time. If you fail, you pick up the pieces, learn from the experience, and move on to the next iteration. In many parts of the world, business cultures value slow, steady progress and failure avoidance.

Time passed. In a conversation I (Linda) had with Sema, an opening appeared. The questions we explored were, "What would the leadership program in Istanbul have allowed for? What is the future that those twenty inspired women leaders would have created?"

Some of the participants would have become facilitators of classes that trained more women. Others would have brought a new level of philanthropy to Turkey. University women would have found their voices, empowered to bring equity in pay and jobs. The picture that Sema painted was compelling. Suddenly, there were those fateful words, "Why not make that your own initiative?" That is just what Sema decided to do.

With a new project in front of her, Sema was filled with self-doubt. She had felt safe in a big corporation like Mattel. She had a wealthy family behind her when, years earlier, she had built the Turkish space camp into a multi-cultural camp for youth from all over the world. What did she know about psychology? About surviving in the academic world? About bridging cultural differences? About giving young women the courage to take on new societal roles?

This is when her friend and mentor, Jeanne Niedorf, stepped into the picture. She brought the expertise. She fully embraced being a cofounder of the Turkish Women's Initiative. She helped develop a curriculum that would lead young women (many of them the first in their families to attend university) to have more self-confidence, to understand myriad issues, and to create change in their communities. The program became known as the Sparks Program.

Sparks Program

The organization that Sema and Jeanne founded—the Turkish Women's Initiative and its corresponding Turkish organization, Degisim Liderleri Dernegi (DLD)—are moving into their thirteenth year. Close to 5400 women have graduated from the Sparks program. It engages women attending universities about becoming leaders and taking on their roles in society. In 2020–21, as a virtual program during the pandemic, they are able to reach more than fifty additional young women.

Sema is proud of the fact that while only 32 percent of Turkish women who start studying at Turkish universities eventually graduate, 100 percent of Sparks program graduates do. About 50 percent of Turkish women who are university graduates are not employed in the labor force—but the majority of Sparks Program graduates are. In addition, the philanthropic projects that are a required part of the curriculum have touched the lives of tens of thousands of people.

Projects in the 2020–21 school year included the creation of an application that can be used to correct gender bias language in documents. In the Turkish language there are two words for woman. One is highly derogatory. The other is not. A cohort of eight women is creating a dictionary that can parse these kinds of inadvertent slurs.

Turning Failure into Success

What is behind the story of Sema creating her own initiative? First of all, while we have a great deal of expertise at formulating plans, it is highly unlikely that absolutely everything will go as we envision. Of course, roadblocks tend to come as surprises, something we did not anticipate. Our immediate reaction to these roadblocks, these breakdowns, is to place blame on ourselves or others. We can easily go down a dark tunnel to feeling like a failure.

What if these roadblocks, these interruptions, are a good sign? What if, in fact, the bigger the vision, the more likely that there will be roadblocks? Instead of blame, we can dispassionately look at the facts. We can answer questions like:

+ What happened?

+ What were the unforeseen conditions?

+ Where is the learning from this situation?

Once everyone is back on the same page (out of blame), it is time to examine commitments. What were we committed to that was blocked? Do we still have the same commitment? Finally, once the commitment is firmly in place, it is time to explore the possibilities we perhaps did not see before. Then, and only then, is it time to take new steps toward our vision.

APPRECIATIVE INQUIRY QUESTIONS TO PONDER

Discover

✓ When in your life did you turn a failure into a success? Did you dispassionately identify what you learned from it?

Dream

✓ What possibilities did you see once you recommitted to the goal?

Design

✓ How was the design influenced by the breakdown that occurred?

Deliver

✓ Continue to recognize breakdowns in your life and keep redesigning from your commitment.

CHAPTER 18

Haunted by Their Stories

WHEN I (LINDA) VISITED KOLKATA, I met Smarita Sengupta, the executive director of Destiny Reflection, at her office. She called all the young women at the facility together so I could meet them. They had all spent time in the sex trade and were now learning to sew to support themselves. They appeared much older than their actual age; the hardships of their lives were painted on their faces. Smarita went around the room and introduced each one. As Smarita had suggested, I brought along their favorite candy and had fun getting them to guess my age in exchange for the coveted prize. They politely guessed less than half of what my gray hair indicated!

Smarita's website describes Destiny's mission "to educate, employ and empower vulnerable children and women in Kolkata so they can avoid sexual exploitation. Our work is about survivor rehabilitation and the prevention of re-trafficking of survivors." The Destiny Reflection website continues with this description of the problem they are addressing:

> Modern slavery is a global problem that every country is affected by. It encompasses sex and labor trafficking, as well as many other forms. The latest estimates reveal that there are more than 40 million victims across the world. There is no possible way to accurately know the number

of victims of modern slavery, but numbers are on the rise. The United Nations has recognized some of the various forms of trafficking and preventing slavery to be a part of the UN Sustainable Development Goals.

Kolkata is the state capital of West Bengal in east India. The city is a major international human trafficking hub. Known as the City of Joy, Kolkata also struggles with poverty. In large slum areas and smaller private brothels in richer suburbs, women work illegally due to the lack of economic opportunities.[60]

Destiny's Work to End Slavery

Over the last two decades, Destiny has helped thousands of women gain freedom from their lives in slavery. Destiny has built partnerships with universities in ten countries. Student ambassadors are frequent visitors and workers in their facilities. Through their e-commerce website and their partners, they have sold more than 50,000 products—beautiful bags and other items made from old saris. Not only are the products part of the learning experience, but they also fund Destiny's work.

Smarita knows that to gain freedom from slavery requires more than just escaping the brothels. It means a change in mindset and economic circumstances. Through literacy programs for improving language skills, training in how to sew garments, arts and crafts sessions, and even mentoring on how to manage money, Destiny assists the survivors in building self-confidence and economic sustainability. Their Khidderpore Red Light Community Center is a dream come true for Smarita's sister, Jayeeta. She wanted a place for the women with children to feel safe while studying with Destiny.

Stories That Will Not Leave Her Mind

Smarita says that she is haunted by the stories of some of the women she has met. Here is one of those stories about "Pahi" (a fictitious name to protect her identity).

Pahi, from Kathmandu, Nepal, was enticed to leave her village with a false assurance of a job in India at the age of fourteen. Once in the neighboring country, she was sold to a brothel in Kolkata's Munshiganj red light area. Because her "master" paid a lot of money to purchase her, she never received any compensation for her labor. Sometimes, if customers were impressed, she would receive a small gratuity.

For the first five years, she was under strict vigilance. She had frequent thoughts about escaping. Such thoughts were futile since she was in a different country, speaking a different language, and without any money. She had no education and often found it hard to read and comprehend even an address. Once she was allowed to go out in the neighborhood, she found many girls from her region facing the same circumstances and gradually made a few friends.

Destiny workers met Pahi when they opened their community center right in the Munshiganj red light area. At that time, Pahi had already been in the trade for more than twenty years. She possessed a strong personality and seemed different from other women in the area. She rejected being pitied and never appreciated people feeling sorry for her. Moreover, she had high self-esteem, which was evident when she asked for favors from people.

She used to speak very little. When she first visited the center, she had a desire to learn alphabets, mostly the English one. She was also keen to be in association with other women and the workers from Destiny to learn about life outside the red-light area.

After several visits, she felt safe enough to tell her story to Smarita. She compared herself to a lipstick in some store where people could buy the product and use it. They could take control of her body, mind, and life as a whole. She felt helpless because she had no skills. She knew nothing except what she had been doing for those many years.

She spoke of deep hatred toward her traffickers. She resented the fact that they never got caught or punished. When thinking and talking about her trafficker, her thoughts turned to violence and revenge.

Pahi finished all the levels of the Destiny literacy program. Destiny appointed her as a preliminary level English teacher to work with the new students and their alphabets. She gained confidence and was extremely happy with her achievement as well as her ability to read addresses. A faint hope for a life of dignity and respect beyond the trade began to glow.

She invented a business with a unique business model. She would travel to Kathmandu to buy products and then return to sell them to other Kolkata brothels. Secondhand garments were one favorite. Another was Wai Wai—a type of instant noodle made in Nepal. She gradually built a customer base. Unfortunately, her business fell on hard times and closed. At that point, the pull of a familiar community was too great. She went back to the Munshiganj area and became employed as a brothel manager. There, she could be with her long-term friends.

Smarita's mind keeps asking questions about Pahi and others like her. Why did they return to those conditions? How can she become a manager in a system she hates? What was missing in the Destiny platform to keep her out of slavery for the rest of her life? Why? Why? Why?

We tend to want the dark side of life to be behind us. We want everything to be tied up in a beautiful bow, to have everyone "live happily ever after" like our childhood fairy tales. Unfortunately, life is more complex than the fairy tales portray. Because of the work Smarita is passionate about, she is exposed to more than her fair share of life's dark moments.

What Can Be Learned from Stories Like Pahi's?

The woman who returned to the brothel was not the same person who left it. The circumstances of the body can be different from those of the mind. Pahi knew more about her own capacity. Destiny had given her an opportunity to identify that potential. She could learn and teach others. She had found an inner strength to start a business from nothing. She had stepped out of the box that society had trapped her in and became, even for a few moments, who she really is. Moments like that are not common. They do not happen every day. Moments like that need to be celebrated and remembered, not left behind.

Smarita had a similar transformation in 2010. Smarita recalls that she went to that program with secret aspirations. These were aspirations that no one had ever told her she could achieve and that she had related to only a few people.

She says that the aspirations were hazy and vague at the beginning of the class. Growing up, she had been bothered by discrimination, social status, and seeing extreme poverty. Her family encouraged a foundation of ethics and respect for other people's emotions that she holds to this day. In the Women Leaders for the World program, she came to believe in her own ability to create opportunities for people. She became a changemaker. She was the one who could actually bring about the changes in Kolkata.

She found out that her dreams and aspirations were not unrealistic. She grew her strength to fight. Her dream expanded. She knew she had a right to live toward her dream. The other participants in her cohort became a professional network unlike any she had experienced. It was her community of support.

What Leadership Lesson Is Evident in These Stories?

Bestselling author Michael Singer has a video course called "The Mind Can Be a Dangerous Place or a Great Gift."[61] In this course, he is differentiating "*The* Mind" from the being that can hear the mind thinking inside our heads. He says that the mind is a collection of all our learnings and all our experiences. The way the mind thinks determines the quality of our lives. Chapter 1 described this collection as the "context" of our lives.

It is possible to shift context through empowering interpretations. Both Smarita and Pahi adopted powerful interpretations of *their own capability*. They shifted some of their negative thoughts to more positive beliefs. They allowed their real selves to shine through, if only for a short while in the case of Pahi.

They found a "best friend" in their minds. That best friend encouraged them. That best friend told them that they could dream and, indeed, that they could make that dream a reality.

And what of the "gifts" of Smarita's mind? Through her vision for Destiny Reflection and decades of her hard work as well as her family's, thousands of women enjoy freedom. As these mothers leave slavery, they also break the chain of enslavement for their children. Despite poverty and struggles, living a life of freedom is, indeed, a precious gift.

APPRECIATIVE INQUIRY QUESTIONS TO PONDER

▦ *Discover*

✓ Do you have an aspiration, a strong desire to achieve something that you have told to only a few people?

✓ When might your aspiration have begun? What might have caused you to long for that change?

▦ *Dream*

✓ Write a page about your aspiration and the strength you have to move toward it.

▦ *Design*

✓ Close your eyes and picture your aspiration when it is fully developed.

▦ *Deliver*

✓ What actions will you regularly focus on to fulfill your aspiration?

CHAPTER 19

The Girls Will Hate Me

WHAT IS THE HARDEST PART of being a leader? Is it living up to widely held expectations like leaders should:

+ Always know "what" to do.

+ Craft perfect project plans.

+ Never make mistakes.

Is it knowing exactly what to do? Not really. There are usually many options to achieve a particular outcome. Is it the difficulty of crafting a project plan? This skill can be learned through widely available project management classes and tools. Is it never making mistakes? If everything had to be perfectly done all the time, we probably would never get started. Give up? Or was it obvious?

The hardest part of being a leader is overcoming your own limitations, especially fear.

Hellen Nkuraiya was mentioned in the introduction to this book. She is a young, petite Maasai woman. The Maasai is an African tribe that lives in Kenya and Tanzania. They are sometimes called the "soul of Africa."[62] They are known as proud warriors.

Hellen certainly showed courage when she traveled to California to attend Women Leaders for the World (WLW) program and when she rescued young Kenyan women from female genital mutilation (FGM). Hellen did what she did despite her deep-seated fear. What did she have to fear? She might have had some obvious fears in the circumstances, such as not raising enough money to feed the girls, being discovered, and being beaten by the girls' parents or having one of the girls "rescued" and taken away.

No, her fear was that the girls would hate her for rescuing them from this horrible tradition that "protected" their virginity but brought on lifelong suffering. The girls might not be able to find a husband because they did not have their physical proof of this "rite of passage."

Hellen had not let a fear of going to the United States stop her from applying to the program. Instead, she adopted a mood of ambition. She would attend the program and be able to rescue more girls—and perhaps even begin to change the tradition in her village.

During the WLW program, she found that her fear about the girls was something that, while it might be a valid concern, was, indeed, something she had invented. She discovered that she had the freedom to create a more "empowering" assumption about what the girls would feel for her in the coming years. She looked into the future and saw them being able to have many children because their reproductive systems had not been damaged. Forming more empowering interpretations is an example of how Hellen learned self-empowerment.

How Can We Lessen Our Fears?

Fears are natural thoughts and reactions to circumstances. They often emanate from assumptions and/or interpretations that may or may not be valid. In Hellen's case, the idea that the young women would not be able to find husbands because of their more "natural" condition was not based on a series of facts. The FGM tradition had been almost universal in her village. She was not inventing a fear out of thin air. To her it was very real, and it was keeping her from expanding her work. Once she had identified the fear and voiced it in a room with others she trusted, it seemed less powerful.

Here is a way to expose and move beyond fears that are getting in the way of fulfilling your vision. Spend time thinking about your vision and what it looks like when you have made progress toward it. What comes into your mind almost immediately will probably be all the roadblocks to accomplishing that progress:

✦ *I am not (fill in the blank: good, rich, or strong) enough to accomplish this.*

✦ *I do not have (fill in the blank: the money, the time, or the talent) to do this.*

✦ *(Insert name) will not love me anymore if I pursue this.*

✦ *(Fill in the blank) has never been done before and looks impossible.*

Now take a hard look at your fears. Certainly, they all seem real to you. Are they, however, based on irrefutable data or are they opinions? Have you had similar fears in the past and been able to overcome them? Can you think of one of your sheroes or heroes who probably had fears like yours but overcame them to go on to success?

Talk to a friend about your vision and your fears. Ask them to help you identify what the facts really are and how you might take a baby step toward your vision. You might invent a skit that pokes fun at your fear.

Living a life where you are pursuing what you care about through fulfilling your vision is more important than your fears. Becoming self-empowered to make conscious choices about your life is an irreplaceable leadership skill.

> *"Courage is not the absence of fear, but*
> *rather the assessment that something*
> *else is more important than fear."*
>
> —Franklin D. Roosevelt

APPRECIATIVE INQUIRY QUESTIONS TO PONDER

Discover

✓ Think of a time in the past when you overcame a fear. What brought you the courage to move ahead despite your fear?

Dream

✓ Identify a current fear and one or more of the assumptions that underpin it. Are they true or just opinions? What is a shift in an assumption that gives you separation from the fear?

✓ Visualize how the future will look when you overcome the fear.

Design

✓ Write two to three empowering interpretations that will allow you to create this future.

Deliver

✓ If you notice yourself feeling disempowered, what new actions will you take to renew your ambition?

PART SIX

Building and Becoming

CHAPTER 20

I Am Not a One-Well Man

MOST OF THE PREVIOUS CHAPTERS HAVE dealt with individuals as leaders acting with their teams. This chapter makes a shift to focus on leaders building communities. Communities come in many shapes and sizes. Peter Block, one of the top authorities on community, says, "Community exists for the sake of belonging and takes its identity from the gifts, generosity, and accountability of its citizens. It is not defined by its fears, its isolation, or its penchant for retribution. We currently have all the capacity, expertise, programs, leaders, regulations, and wealth required to end unnecessary suffering and create an alternative future."[63]

By this definition, *community* is the essence of an effective team. What if being part of a community can be:

+ The core of a thriving life?

+ A continuous feeling of connectedness, support, and empowerment?

+ A source of unimagined resources?

+ A limitless feeling of belonging?

All these are possible when certain fundamentals are present in a community.

Building a Community

Sabore Ole Oyie is a Maasai warrior and elder in his tribe. What was he doing attending a "women's" leadership program in California? In 2010, the Global Women's Leadership Network partnered with the Santa Clara University School of Law to cocreate the annual leadership program. Cynthia Mertens of the law school insisted that if it was going to be about justice, it had to be gender blind! The name was changed to Global Leaders for Justice, and *voila,* three men attended.

Sabore is an imposing male standing almost seven feet tall. He wears traditional Maasai warrior robes and, on occasion, carries a *large* sword. (This really impresses the youth audiences he addresses.) His "impossible" project to promote justice in his village was to build a well. Not an easy task given the topography of his region. Having a well close to the village would mean that the mothers would not have to walk miles every day to carry water back to their homes.

According to the website Lifewater.org, "nearly 800 million people lack access to clean water."[64] Their definition is "access to safe water in under 30 minutes round trip." In the same article, they name the top-ten countries lacking this basic resource. Eight of those are African countries.

In a mid-2017 blog, *The Conversation* talks about the consequences of using unsafe water. They say, "A sufficient supply of biologically and chemically safe water is necessary for drinking and personal hygiene to prevent diarrheal diseases, trachoma, intestinal worm infections, stunted growth among children and numerous other deleterious outcomes from chemical contaminants like arsenic and lead." The article went on further to state that "In a study of 25 countries in sub-Saharan Africa, UNICEF estimated that women there spent 16 million hours collecting water each day."[65]

Obviously, proximity and access to safe drinking water would bring both health and equity to Sabore's village.

On the third day of the Global Leaders seminar, Sabore asked to speak after a coffee break. He stood up to his full height and pronounced that his project had changed. He had been listening to others in the class speaking about their commitments to end human trafficking, feed the hungry of an entire country, etc. He proudly announced that "I am not a one-well man! I will bring wells to all the villages in the region."

Sabore's story and vision were compelling. The first set of funds he received was from a seventeen-year-old high school student who was so moved by Sabore's description of the fate of the women in his community that she handed him three crumpled-up five-dollar bills. It was through teaching American youth about the importance of water that the donations started to come in.

A vision and donations were insufficient to achieve his goal, however. That would require him to step into building an international community.

The Fundamentals of Community Building

The first fundamental is *listening* to others in the community. While communities have designated leaders, everyone in the community has a contribution to make. When a space is generated for everyone to express their ideas, more can be accomplished. There is a deep respect for what others are saying in effective communities. People feel heard. There may even be long silences as people digest what someone has just said.

The second fundamental is *trust*. People grant trust from different bases. Trust is influenced by both personal and cultural values. Some people tend to trust people who are competent. Others need to know they can rely on someone. Still others grant trust to those who they believe have integrity—those keeping promises, following through, and telling the truth.

Third, for a community to grow beyond the sum of its members, there is a commitment to an *integration of ideas*. Like a beautiful French braid, it is about expertly weaving ideas to create results. Through communication and dedication, new possibilities are born in a community.

Fourth, communities bring *value* to their members. One major benefit of being part of a healthy community is learning from others. As a member of a community, one learns from, is nurtured by, and contributes to the whole. When one becomes part of another community, there is a transfer of knowledge between the communities through the mutual members.

Fifth, when one is part of a well-conceived community, one experiences a feeling of *being invited* instead of commanded to join. One wants to be with the other members both to create results and to feel valued.

Sabore used all these fundamentals to achieve his vision. In Kenya, he built a modern-day community around his well. People, mostly from California and Oregon, have come to see the progress of the drilling. The local community embraced these visitors and through the interactions with them grew to be more global.

Once the well was functioning, the women gathered daily to pump water. While their journey was shorter, it still involved carrying heavy containers of water to their homes. This meant that they left their young children behind when they came to the well. Thérèse Hjelm, an American woman who had partnered with Sabore throughout the process of building the well, saw the possibility to provide a preschool for the young ones. More fundraising followed, particularly from educators in the United States. More visits were made to view the progress on the school buildings. Today, Naretu Academy has three classes and seventy-six young Maasai students. The school and the well are the center of the community.

A Wide Variety of Communities

Most people, like Sabore who belongs to local and international communities, belong to several groups at any point in their lives. There are many types of communities based on:

+ Desire to learn like study groups in college

+ Common interests like bridge clubs

+ One's profession like ancient guilds of masons

+ Religious beliefs.

A common type of community in business, civil society, academia, and government is one formed to achieve a common commitment. This community of commitment shares a vision and a promise to act toward that vision.

As mentioned in the previous chapter, the Global Women's Leadership Network (GWLN) was formed around visions and coordinated actions. Through numerous conversations in which individual visions for the future of the organization were discussed, a common vision emerged. GWLN imagined women who would be whole as women and whole as leaders dedicated to a whole world. The team focused on increasing leadership capacity to improve the lives of communities around the world.

The first year of the organization, GWLN was not a network. It started life as a "center." This is a popular term in academic circles and the organization began at a university— Santa Clara University in California. Their first leadership class was held in their second year of existence. The name they gave to the class was Women Leaders for the World (WLW).

During the first class, it became apparent that the organization would be more successful if leadership was shared with the class participants. The concept of being a network was born. The first class and the founders became a community that supported each other far beyond the short time of being together in California. A ceremony held at each graduation symbolized the community effect. Each fellow was given a cream-colored candle with the inscription:

WHOLE WOMAN
WHOLE LEADER
WHOLE WORLD

A "master" candle was used to light all the new fellows' candles. The graduation was often a public event with volunteers, donors, and friends present. Smaller candles were handed out to everyone and lighted by the new fellows passing among the crowd. Often, one of the fellows (some of whom had wonderful voices) would lead everyone in a song such as "We Rise."* There was not a dry eye in the room as everyone blew out their candles.

Over succeeding years, stories came back from around the world of how the fellows used their original candle as a master in their own community ceremonies. There is even a term that sociologists use now for these kind of rituals: *collective effervescence.*

Five Steps to Creating Vibrant Communities

What can a leader do to build or strengthen a community, particularly communities of commitment? How can a leader encourage people to not only join communities but also to contribute to them?

1. *Create a welcoming and safe space for people.*

When people feel welcomed and safe, they will participate, voice ideas, and cocreate the space. People's experience is shaped by the way they are brought together, and the way conversations are framed and reframed.

---

* Here is a link to Maame Yelbert Obeng singing this song at a later event: "Maame Afon RISE (Inspirational music by US-based Ghana-born Gospel Artiste)," Maame Afon, August 9, 2012, video, 6:17, https://www.youtube.com/watch?v=SpXTFherY5E.

As mentioned, people like to be invited to join in, not told to attend. Since everyone's time is valuable and there are many choices where to spend one's time, community organizers are constantly asking, "What can we create together that we could not create alone?" The answer to this question is often at the heart of the value that people are looking for in joining any group.

Here is an example of a community fashioned on an ancient tradition: One of the programs of the Global Women's Leadership Network was called "At the Well." Like women all over the world who congregated to talk where they collected water, this program was about an open dialogue on life's issues. One person would tell a story about their personal journey to seed the conversation. The person was encouraged to be vulnerable and talk about their challenges as well as their triumphs. During the session, three questions were posed and discussed around the circle. The final question was always about action—what different action was each person going to take because of what they learned that day?

2. Listen without judgment.

While listening with filters like "What do I like/not like about this" and "Do I agree/disagree with what is being said" are natural for human beings, building community requires one to set these normal ways of listening aside. Leading by listening without judgment affirms and enhances everyone's capacity to contribute. Putting aside assumptions and expectations, the mind is fertile ground for planting seeds—diverse ways of thinking are encouraged. Listening without judgment is the basis for respect. Fostering each person being accepted just as they are helps people to unite as one.

3. *Generate common bonds through the community's stories.*

Stories are born from common experiences. When these stories are voiced in the broader community, common bonds are strengthened. What a community is capable of is codified through its stories. When the community's stories contain not only facts but also the feelings experienced, community members become a part of the triumphs and even the failures at a different level. They are connected at the head and the heart. The stories truly live.

5. *Promote feelings of value, of being recognized, and of caring.*

Community members can be paid employees, like in corporations, or volunteers like in many civil society organizations. In both cases, they have the same needs—to feel valued, to be recognized, and to feel that the organization cares for them. Barry Posner and Jim Kouzes, two of the most well-known authors on the subject leadership, wrote a book entitled *Encouraging the Heart* that espouses making recognition personal. In the book, they share a story about Wayne Bennette, who ceremonially attached an employee's recognition check to the machine used by that worker. This illustrates the caring creativity that can come into play when recognizing someone's efforts and making them feel valued.[66]

5. *Define clear rules of engagement.*

Some people believe that accountability to an organization is generated by being paid. If this were true, every for-profit entity would run like clockwork. Accountability is essentially a part of culture that must be purposely implanted. When volunteers or employees know what is expected of them and see accountability modeled by the "leaders," they are more likely to become engaged. Add to that feeling connected to the mission and empowered to act—and accountability can blossom!

Accountability is a chain of requests and promises. A complete request contains not only the task being requested but also any other terms and conditions that apply. One of these terms is always a "when" this task needs to be completed. Vague, oblique, and other indirect forms of requests leave others in the community confused.

Promises are the response to a request. One can accept the request, decline the request, or counter the request—modifying its form or due date. In some communities, declines are discouraged or even "taboo." This leads to misunderstandings about commitments and, usually, missed deadlines.

APPRECIATIVE INQUIRY QUESTIONS TO PONDER

▨ Discover

✓ What is one community you belong to where you experience the feeling of trust?

▨ Dream

✓ Where do you want to form a new community or strengthen a current one?

▨ Design

✓ What value(s) can this community bring to its members?

▨ Deliver

✓ What actions can you take to keep or make the community vibrant and thriving?

CHAPTER 21

The Pencil Is in Your Hands

AbilityPath, a nonprofit social enterprise located on the San Francisco Peninsula, is entering its second century of operation. It has "one of the most comprehensive service portfolios spanning all ages from early intervention for infants to community access and job training for adults and seniors. All programs are designed to prepare children and adults to actively participate in their schools, communities, workplaces, and at home."[67] AbilityPath promotes acceptance, respect, and inclusion for those with disabilities.

Bryan Neider, the CEO, is a former top executive from Electronic Arts. He is using his extensive leadership skills at AbilityPath because he believes that everyone should have a place in the community. I (Linda) met Bryan when he was a guest speaker in my MBA class called "A C-Level Perspective" at Santa Clara University. He always impressed the students with his emphasis on people. He believed that a focus on your people was as important as, if not more important than, a focus on activities.

Erin Montgomery, the vice president of human resources at AbilityPath, spent many of her younger years working in high tech, the engine of Silicon Valley. She has now spent over a decade at AbilityPath developing people and building an organization that assists those with disabilities to find greater independence. We met Erin when we became involved in offering a transformational leadership education seminar for AbilityPath executives. Erin later became a certified trainer for all our courses.

An Email Starts the Process

It all began with an email from us to Bryan. We had finalized a new leadership curriculum called "You as a Leader." It was a three-day seminar plus six months of coaching that explored the leader within and how, when that authentic leader was brought to the office, a new level of teamwork could be created. Would Bryan and AbilityPath (then called Gatepath) be the pilot?

Synchronicity played a part at this juncture. Bryan and Erin had been considering leadership training for the coming year. Bryan had already engaged the organization in a vision process. A huge mural of their vision filled their main conference room. Over the years, Bryan had come to trust me (Linda) and my abilities in the leadership realm as an executive professor at the Leavey School of Business. He bravely asked all his senior managers to join him at the seminar.

They explored the way they listen to each other, the questions they ask, what they each care most deeply about, and how they wanted to relate to each other and their employees. A highlight was their depiction, in a series of skits, of the stories that most represented their culture. All charities are scarce in resources, but when Bryan and several other executives showed up mouthing a recording of Linda Ronstadt's "Poor, Poor, Pitiful Me," they not only brought down the house, but broke the back of that corporate paradigm.

The improvements in communication and results convinced Bryan and Erin to invite all their managers to similar sessions. Bryan and Erin were true role models, one of them kicking off each session. A common language and common team-building actions spread.

Scaling the Initiative

How could this be spread cost-effectively across the whole organization, including their youthful volunteers? "Everyone a Leader" was a co-creation between Erin and us. The managers who had attended three days became coaches for the one-day program graduates.

Bryan, Erin, and all the employees ushered in a new, more inclusive culture that fostered individual and team innovation. That attitude of innovation led to two organizations, Gatepath and Abilities United, being merged into AbilityPath. The entire senior management team from both organizations was involved in another leadership workshop to foster teamwork and to plan the future of the new entity. Senior management asked their board of directors to help them be better, to help them evolve.

Diversity, Equity, and Inclusion (DEI) Explored

Fast forward a few years to when the George Floyd case swept the nation. Bryan and Erin did not just see this as a newspaper headline, a tragic event that happened far away. They felt it was a call to action for themselves and their organization. It called for them to reexamine the meaning of inclusion. They decided to look beyond the dictionary definition into what inclusion really meant for them. That quest for clarity turned into a fascinating (and continuing) journey.

For some time, AbilityPath had been about creating a place where people with developmental disabilities could belong— where everyone has a place. This meant parents inviting kids with special needs to birthday parties with their other children at a location called Grins & Giggles. It meant building skills in young adults so that they could work in the community at supermarkets, drugstores, and restaurants.

Yet, as Erin and Brian dug deeper into diversity, equity, and inclusion (DEI), they found that, for them, it was about how they defined and practiced inclusion as one of their core organizational values. They were viewing inclusion too narrowly, for themselves, AbilityPath's employees, and those they served. They had tough conversations that uncovered their own hidden biases and created space for employees and people served to share their experiences. They found new self-respect and, in turn, respect for others.

They recognized the intersectionality experienced by employees and people with developmental disabilities. There were many different identities represented at AbilityPath: race, ethnicity, gender, sexual orientation, socio-economic background, age, and religion. The exploration challenged them both personally and professionally. It was a catalyst for a cultural shift at the organization. They knew that they had to model what they were discovering and make their actions congruent with **Diversity, Equity, and Inclusion (DEI)**.

They needed to engage with their community to expand inclusion beyond those who came to AbilityPath because a loved one has a developmental disability. They wanted to share the power and impact of inclusion. They wanted to invite others to be a part of it. They discovered that people genuinely wanted to learn about inclusion. Students, volunteers, and partners were attracted to work with an organization that understood this dimension and shared the same values. An inclusive attitude, and the resulting culture, welcomed not only people but also their ideas and life experiences. They embarked on a journey to foster learning. They offered to share what they were learning with a broad spectrum of organizations—for free. AbilityPath recognized that they were at the beginning of their learning journey. They made a commitment to continue this work and to engage others as a core practice. Bryan, Erin, and the entire organization realize that their journey is only beginning.

The Soft Skills Are the Hard Skills

For Bryan and Erin, the hardest work was at an emotional level as they practiced introspection and examined their own privilege and views of the world. They expressed gratitude that their teams joined the learning journey. The teams held space for actively listening and learning. The deeply embedded theme of "everyone a leader" was a key to the buy-in and engagement. Now they called on everyone throughout organization.

They treated their employees with new respect as the global pandemic caused everyone's daily routines to be uprooted. COVID-19 brought stress and hardship. Communication, including continuously asking for input and feedback, made people feel like the organization cared about them and their ideas beyond the year's goals.

Bryan began to speak about the fact that "the pencil to help write our future is in your hands." He engaged people in preparing scenarios for various ways to cope with the curve balls that the pandemic was throwing at them. *What ways could they improve people's health and well-being? How could they migrate many of their highly personal services to online? How could they name their services in a way which represented the people served? How could they bring an equity lens to every program? How could they take what worked during the pandemic and bring it forward into a new future?*

A level of trust and a willingness to take risks came forth in AbilityPath because there were no penalties for mistakes. One new manager was wide-eyed when she was asked to design a complete recreational therapy program for adults. The message was: "You are welcome at the table, and we want you to take on being the leader you are."

The focus on diversity and inclusion is creating a harmonized unity where everyone participates.

It Takes Leadership

Taking on challenges such as diversity, equity, and inclusion is the job of leaders. Such challenges are not theoretical. They are self-reflection exercises that require taking on personal as well as organizational commitments. Shaping culture takes a "not-knowing" mindset, time, and patience. It also takes daring—getting out of your own comfort zone on behalf of a better life for your employees, clients, volunteers, board members, and all those who touch your organization.

APPRECIATIVE INQUIRY QUESTIONS TO PONDER

▨ *Discover*

✓ What communities are you a part of that hold the values of DEI? How are these communities demonstrating DEI?

▨ *Dream*

✓ Envision the opportunities you have to support and encourage DEI in either your community or in a community you will create. What enlivens you about this opportunity?

▨ *Design*

✓ What are two or three different ways you can start to fulfill your dream? What partners will you invite as a part of your design team? In this team, how will you live and demonstrate DEI as you generate your path forward?

▨ *Deliver*

✓ How will you sustain these values as your community works together and becomes visible in the wider world?

CHAPTER 22

Let's Plant Trees Whose Shade We May Never Sit In

EVERY FOUNDER OF AN ORGANIZATION comes to that point where it is time to turn the organization over to the next leadership team. If one is lucky and plans ahead, that transition is smooth and easy. In some instances, it can become traumatic and painful.

From a premonition while standing in a stream to personally meeting almost 200 participants, Women Leaders for the World (WLW) had been my (Linda's) "baby." It was my way of fulfilling the 1866 quote about planting seeds for trees one would never sit under from French theologian Hyacinthe Loyson. Now, moving out of the San Francisco Bay Area loomed on the horizon. It was time to sell our large home in California and settle in a smaller place somewhere less hectic and less expensive for retirement.

Unfortunately, the fundraising had not achieved a level where the organization could be supported by a paid staff—even if only one employee, an executive director. The funds raised, mostly from Bay Area friends, were only adequate to support one annual California program. The fellows' results spoke loudly for more frequent programs. Some board members were calling for classes in developing countries through regional alliances.

It was a wild real estate market. Our house sold quickly at full price, all cash, and sixty days to vacate. The moment had arrived: I had to give up. I resigned. The future of the organization was in the hands of the board and the dedicated volunteers.

Despite being busier than ever being a grandmother (my daughter delivered twins the same month we moved out) and arranging a new life, I felt devastated and disappointed with myself. I was leaving behind the house where I had raised my children and the state where I had lived since entering high school. I was leaving behind the feelings of being in an inspiring community of women leaders from around the world and friendships of fifty-five years. I felt sad and alone. I had entered a major transition in my life.

Becoming More Resilient

Resilience is built by being tested. Life provides challenges. These are natural forces just like gravity and wind. When we stay the course despite the challenges, when we improve on areas of our being that need work, and when we seek honorable pursuits, we become more resilient.

In a conversation with the founder of Enlightened Motivation, Dr. Mehrad Nazari, he said, "Resilience is an attitude. It is a decision, a choice. It is a philosophy of life. You believe deep down that nothing can stop you, particularly when you are following a virtuous action." He continued, "You build resilience with commitment, grit, and tenacity. You must set your mind to it and if it is a virtuous pursuit the universe will support you."[68]

An April 2020 opinion column in the *New York Times* entitled "On Coronavirus Lockdown? Look for Meaning, Not Happiness," Emily Esfahani Smith asked a provocative question: "Is there anything people can do to cope with the emotional fallout of this confusing and challenging time?" Their answer was: cultivate "tragic optimism," a term coined by Viktor Frankl, a Holocaust survivor and author.[69]

Everyone experiences despair, fear, anxiety, and even hopelessness. There is no denial of the effects of a situation like the global pandemic. Yet, in the midst of those emotions, somehow, we find a way to hold on to a glimmer of optimism, to move ahead with life. This is not achieved by eating a gallon of ice cream, sleeping late, or simply putting a fake smile on our face. It is achieved by doing something with meaning like volunteering to help someone less fortunate or being grateful for the love of family. The "good" feeling that comes from these activities invites happy feelings that have a lasting quality.

Resilience in Normal Times

Is resilience needed during normal times? Is it important to cultivate resilience for everyday situations like our office settings? The answer is "yes."

It is easy to fall into unhealthy moods like resentment or resignation that require resilience. We resent something that someone did to us, for instance passing over us for a promotion or not getting the raise we expected. In resentment, we have feelings of anger, loss, helplessness, or sadness. We are a victim. We can become resigned in situations. We have tried to get a task done many times and have failed consistently. We are stuck in the realm of no possibility. We feel hopeless, tired, and disappointed. We are giving up, withdrawing, and stopping our action. When we are in these moods, resilience requires finding our own inner strength as a source of commitment and action.

The first step is recognizing that you are in one of those states. After settling in my Tucson home, I realized that I was in a mood of resignation. There was nothing I could do about the situation. Who am I going to *be* in my retirement?

The second step to shifting out of resignation or resentment is framing a commitment that moves you into action. I recommitted to a world alive with peace, justice, and love.

The third step is generating a long list of possibilities. What organizations locally supported that commitment, especially for women? How could I serve them? What about authoring my own leadership course? Was it time to write the book everyone had been encouraging me to write? With travel curtailed, how could I be close to my growing grandsons?

The fourth step is to act toward one or more of those possibilities. I contacted the local American Association of University Women and volunteered. They needed someone to teach their Start Smart seminars at the University of Arizona. It was a perfect fit for my background as both a businesswoman and a business school professor. I jumped in with both feet.

Resilience takes many forms depending on the situation. The more we recognize that we *are* resilient, the more we will build reserves for use in the most trying times.

Appreciative Inquiry Questions to Ponder

Discover
✓ When have you shown resilience? Recall as many situations as you can.

Dream
✓ Where in your life do you need resilience now?

Design
✓ What would it look like in that part of your life if you build that resilience?

Deliver
✓ What one or two actions can you take to move toward being resilient?

CHAPTER 23

A Seat at the Table

A RECENT *FORBES* ARTICLE SUGGESTS THAT "A more effective way for women to get a seat at the table is to build our own tables."[70] More and more women worldwide are already using this vehicle to become their own boss and overcome societal barriers. This is not a short-term burst. Over the last twenty years, female ownership of business has increased over 114 percent.[71]

Dr. Anita Borg, a computer scientist and cofounder of the respected digital community Systers, dedicated her life to lifting up women in tech. She cofounded the Grace Hopper Celebration and the Institute for Women and Technology (IWT). The latter became the Anita Borg Institute upon her untimely death in 2003. Anita believed that "Women need to assume their rightful place at the table creating the technology of the future."[72]

As a lone woman in tech, she knew that women's ideas were needed to forward the science of information technology and improve the products. Besides assisting with the Grace Hopper Celebration, she was uncertain how to bring more women into computing. Then came her attendance at a very impactful women's leadership course called Leadership for New Futures. The facilitators were Barbara Fittipaldi and Elaine Fox. I (Linda) was in the course with Anita. She had a dream about women's role in forwarding technology. She described this as a "spiraling up" of women's potential to contribute to and build a better world.

Anita's Dream and the Leadership Program

On May 31, 2001, I interviewed Anita Borg. At the time, she was in the initial stages of fighting brain cancer. She told me the story of how her journey to found IWT began.

She recalled being in a conversation with Barbara Fittipaldi in which she was "given permission" to talk about what she really wanted to accomplish. She highlighted the "intense" listening that Barbara gave to her idea. She spoke about an institute for women in technology. She gave this listening credit for her ability to think bigger and bolder.

Her dreams were beyond reasonable. She started to share her vision with others. She thought they were "wild"; others found them compelling.

After a great deal of conversation, Anita enrolled in one of Barbara Fittipaldi's leadership classes. She was not sure how she would benefit from a class that was not technical. That had always been her primary skill set. Soon, her skepticism turned to enthusiasm for the entrepreneurial process. Anita remembered being told, "Don't worry about execution." This gave her permission to move beyond her fear of speaking about something that seemed almost impossible.

She was asked to imagine that she had every resource, all the funding, and all the time to accomplish her vision. She found this to be freeing, even exciting. When she put her grand vision on the mountaintop and planned the steps from the future, it looked a lot more doable. She fell in love with this scenario-planning technique.

Her vision had morphed. Now she knew she "wanted to build a network of networks to connect and support women in technology everywhere." She crafted a proposal asking the National Science Foundation for $6 million. She took other actions. Among these was reading *The Futures of Women: Scenarios for the 21st Century* by Pamela McCorduck and Nancy Ramsey. This laid out alternate futures for women, depending on the impact of societal forces. The scenarios were labeled a golden age of equality, backlash, two steps forward and two steps back, and separate but doing fine. Anita wanted to ensure that the golden age was the one that would occur for technical women.

A Special Brainstorming Session

Elaine and Barbara Fittipaldi pulled together a very special meeting right in Elaine's Princeton, New Jersey, living room. Lots of industries were represented including technology, psychology, television, etc. The two authors of *The Futures of Women* were there. I (Linda) wanted to support Anita and flew east to be part of her brain trust.

This was the meeting where Anita named the organization the Institute for Women in Technology (IWT) and visualized her spiral. The organization was at the center of a diagram with spirals shooting off it to represent projects that were byproducts of her own effort. Money was going to be important. Anita had gotten initial seed funding from the Kellogg Foundation.

I (Linda) was tasked with leading the session on how to finance the organization. We did Anita's favorite "top of the mountain" exercise. I think that we had about $20,000 at the top. As the exercise progressed, I realized that this amount of money was not stimulating any BIG ideas. So, I picked up the marker, marched to the flipchart, and made it $1,000,000. Ideas start popping!

When Anita returned to California, she approached Mark Weiser, a boss at Xerox Parc, with her idea. She believed he would support an idea like this, and he did. John Sealy Brown, the Parc Chief Scientist, agreed with Anita that IWT was a way to improve women's lives and, in turn, improve communities. Because they wanted her to do research for Parc, she agreed to join the organization and accept more seed funding for IWT.

It was at this point that Anita discovered that she had brain cancer. This caused her to become more of a leader and less of a doer. She said, "My struggle with cancer meant that I needed to allow others to contribute. I had to get better at asking for help. The growth of IWT would be dependent on my ability to get other resources working on the vision."

Anita recruited Telle Whitney, a fellow technical woman, to move the project forward. Eventually, Telle became the executive director of IWT.

Thanks to Anita's vision and the years she dedicated to getting it started, the Anita Borg Institute has become a powerful global organization for women technologists. They run the Grace Hopper Celebration in the United States and India, support student academic programs, encourage women to rejoin the workforce through their back-to-work program, do codeathons, and stimulate entrepreneurial ideas. Thousands of women, young and old, are touched by the dream Anita had. Her courage in battling her disease and continuing to build her dream is a model for every leader.

Sometimes, women need to build their own organization to have a seat at the table.

Appreciative Inquiry Questions to Ponder

▪ *Discover*

✓ Find a time in your life when you made your dream bigger. How did it feel?

▪ *Dream*

✓ How would you answer the question, "If I knew I could not fail, what would I take on?" If you pursued this dream, what is an almost impossible outcome you can imagine for two years in the future?

▪ *Design*

✓ Take the outcome from two years in the future and put it at the top of a blank piece of paper. Draw three lines down the page, like the sides of a tent and the tentpole inside. These lines are pathways for accomplishing the outcome. Now, starting from two years in the future, come down one of the legs with actions that answer the recurring question, "What just happened to create that progress?" Complete three pathways that are as different as possible. Be sure that one is totally outlandish!

▪ *Deliver*

✓ Is there an action near the bottom of your diagram that you can take now that starts you toward your dream of reaching the mountaintop?

The Never-Ending Journey to Becoming

BECOMING AN ACCOMPLISHED LEADER, OR AUTHOR, is not a destination; it is a journey. It starts with what one cares about. It is a process of discovery, dreaming, designing, and delivering toward your care. Every one of the leaders in this book led from their care—their heart. Each wanted something special:

+ Alma: provide needed services to Nogales' marginalized population

+ Anita: have women influence technology and the whole technology industry

+ Ashlie: end human trafficking and other forms of human slavery

+ Barbara (Bylenga): have women step into their rightful leadership roles worldwide

+ Barbara (Key): shine her light so others know that life is shaped by cares

+ Bryan and Erin: live the true meaning of inclusion

+ Catherine: bring human dignity and livelihoods to Naivasha's marginalized women

+ Deanna: stimulate women in technology supporting each other

+ Diti: teach youth to protect and cherish nature

+ Florence: inspire ambition in the youth of Tanzania

+ Kathryn: transform the healthcare industry

+ Linda: promote a world alive with peace, justice, and love

+ Lucky: give Nepalese women a chance to succeed

+ Maame: live whole woman, whole leader, whole world

+ Philile and Priya: provide financial freedom for everyone

+ Sabore: support health and equity for women and men in his region

+ Sandhya: allow more baby girls to have joyful lives

+ Sema: promote equity for Turkish women through stepping into leadership

+ Smarita: create livelihoods and education for Indian women leaving the sex trade

Every one of them was open to new ways of leading. Every one of them was tested to the core by challenging experiences. Every one of them learned from their sometimes-painful experiences who they were at their core. As Barry so eloquently said in his foreword, the people in this book had "something that they held dear, were willing to fight for, to suffer and sacrifice for, to grieve if lost and to shout with joy when achieved." Every one of them had resilience. Every one of them is a loving human being and loves being a social change leader.

In their treatise *Leading from the Emerging Future,* Otto Scharmer and Katrin Kaufman seem to capture the essence of these new leaders. They said:

> Go to the edges of the self. To apply this process in the context of institutions, we have to power it with a new leadership technology. The core of this technology focuses on tuning three instruments: the open mind, the open heart, and the open will. With an open mind, we can suspend old habits of thought. With an open heart, we can empathize, or see a situation through the eyes of someone else. With an open will, we can let go and let the new come.[73]

It is time for the world to recognize and accept everyone can be a leader. Everyone can bring energy and compassion. Everyone is capable of creating innovative solutions to complex problems.

Women Leaders for the World (WLW) started with one leader who believed in herself and who received the support she needed from a university dean. With each cohort, the network of social activists grew. Their efforts fostered hundreds and, eventually, thousands of others who know that leadership springs from within. This book honors every individual who speaks from the heart and acts in concert with their deepest values.

*"When you let go of who you are,
you become who you might be."*

—Rumi

Leadership Sheroes and Heroes

Alma Cota de Yanez, Directora, FESAC Fundacion del Empresariado Sonorense AC Capitulo Nogales, Mexico, https://www.linkedin.com/in/alma-cota-de-yanez-21423b10b/

Anita Borg, computer scientist and Co-founder of the Institute for Women and Technology and the Grace Hopper Celebration of Women in Computing. https://en.wikipedia.org/wiki/Anita_Borg (deceased)

Ashlie Bryant, CEO and Co-Founder 3Strands Global, El Dorado Hills, CA, https://www.linkedin.com/in/ashlie-bryant-60816129/

Barbara Bylenga, Founder, and Executive Director of SHE-CAN, https://www.linkedin.com/in/barbara-bylenga-252466/

Barbara Key, authoress, consultant, coach, and teacher, https://www.linkedin.com/in/barbara-key-989622/

Barbara Fittipaldi, CIO SpotTheLine, https://www.linkedin.com/in/barbara-fittipaldi-a996b111/

Barry Posner, PhD, Professor of Leadership, ex-Dean of the Leavey School of Business at Santa Clara University, author of

The Leadership Challenge, and consultant, https://www.linkedin.com/in/barryp1/

Bryan Neider, CEO AbilityPath, https://www.linkedin.com/in/bryan-neider-92016b/

Catherine Wanjohi, Founder and Executive Director, LifeBloom Services, transformative leadership coach/mentor, and author https://www.linkedin.com/in/catherine-wanjohi-06aa4735/

Deanna Kosaraju, Founder/CEO at Global Tech Women, https://www.linkedin.com/in/deanna-kosaraju-138922/

Diti Mookherjee, CEO, Association for Social and Environmental Development, Kolkata, India, https://www.linkedin.com/in/diti-mookherjee/

Erin Montgomery, Vice President of Human Resources, https://www.linkedin.com/in/ermontgomery/

Florence Temu, Country Director, AMREF Tanzania, https://www.linkedin.com/in/temu-dr-florence-06ba763/

Hellen Nkuraiya, Maasai village leader and teacher, https://adventure.com/maasai-tourism-women-empowerment-kenya/

Julie Castro Abrams, Founder and CEO, How Women Lead, https://www.linkedin.com/in/julie-castro-abrams/

Kathryn Johnson, Hospital and Healthcare Consultant, https://www.linkedin.com/in/kathryn-johnson-a833304/

Linda Alepin, leadership author and consultant, former F 200 executive, retired Executive Professor and past president, AAUW Tucson, https://www.linkedin.com/in/lindaalepin/

Lucky K. Chhetri, Founder/Director of 3 Sisters Adventure Trekking & Empowering Women of Nepal (EWN), Nepal, https://www.linkedin.com/in/lucky-chhetri-2a30056/. Among many honors is being an Ashoka Fellow 2004.

M. Thérèse Hjelm, cofounder Sabore's Well, https://sabore-swell.org/team-1

Mehrad Nazari, PhD, author, Speaker + Founder Enlightened Negotiation®, San Diego County, CA, https://www.linkedin.com/in/drmehradnazari/

Maame Afon Yelbert-Sai, Chief Steward @MILT Strategy & Relationship Architect Leadership Impact Coach and Mentor, https://www.linkedin.com/in/maame-afon-aba-yelbert-sai-a649173a/

Mary Burns, President at the Kasimu Education Foundation, https://www.linkedin.com/in/mary-burns-1275699/ (deceased)

Pat Obuchowski, author of *Gutsy Women Win*, https://www.linkedin.com/in/patobuchowski/

Phionah Musumba, Founder and Executive Director, Malkia Foundation, https://www.linkedin.com/in/phionah-musumba-50b4007b/

Priya Thakoor, Managing Executive: Digital Channels at Vodacom, https://www.linkedin.com/in/priyathakoor/

Philile Mkhize, Technology Divisional Executive - Corporate Functions at Liberty Group South Africa, https://www.linkedin.com/in/philile-mkhize/

Sabore Ole Oyie, Maasai Warrior and Elder, https://sabore-swell.org/team-1

Sandhya Puchalapalli, President, Vijay Foundation Trust, https://www.linkedin.com/in/sandhya-puchalapalli-97b13512/

Sema Basol, Co-founder, Turkish Women's Initiative, https://www.linkedin.com/in/sema-basol-44a6283/

Smarita Sengupta, Founder, Destiny Foundation, https://www.linkedin.com/in/smarita-sengupta/

References

Basol, Sema, interviewed by the authors, April 4, 2021

Borg, Anita, interviewed by the authors, May 17, 2001

Bryant, Ashlie, interviewed by the authors, April 21, 2021

Bylenga, Barbara, interviewed by the authors (part II), March 23, 2021

Chhetri, Lucky, interviewed by the authors, February 17, 2021

Cota de Yanez, Alma, interviewed by the authors, August 1, 2020

Johnson, Kathryn, interviewed by the authors, July 7, 2020

Kosaraju, Deanna, interviewed by the authors, February 18, 2021

Mkhize, Philile, and Thakoor, Priya, interviewed by the authors, March 10, 2021

Montgomery, Erin, and Neider, Bryan, interviewed by the authors, February 23, 2021

Mookherjee, Diti, interviewed by the authors, July 31, 2020

Musumba, Phionah, interviewed by the authors, March 18, 2021

Nazari, Mehrad, interviewed by the authors, September 8, 2020

Sengupta, Smarita, interviewed by the authors, March 25, 2021

Temu, Florence, interviewed by the authors, August 10, 2020

Wanjohi, Catherine, interviewed by the authors, July 15, 2020

Yelbert-Sai, Maame Afon Aba, interviewed by the authors, November 18, 2020

Institute for Generative Leadership: www.generateleadership.com

Strozzi Institute: www.strozziinstitute.com

Endnotes

1 Tom Moon, "The Story of Marvin Gaye's 'What's Going On,'" NPR. org, August 7, 2000, https://www.npr.org/2000/08/07/1080444/ npr-100-whats-going-on.

2 United Nations, "COVID-19's Far Reaching Impact on Global Drug Abuse," *UN News*, June 25, 2020, https://news.un.org/en/story/2020/ 06/1066992.

3 Mimiko, Oluwafemi, *Globalization: The Politics of Global Economic Relations and International Business*, (Durham, N.C.: Carolina Academic Press, 2012), 47.

4 Lifewater, "9 World Poverty Statistics that Everyone Should Know," Lifewater blog, January 28, 2020, https://lifewater.org/blog/9-world -poverty-statistics-to-know-today/.

5 Leslie E Sekerka, *Ethics is a Daily Deal: Choosing to Build Moral Strength as a Practice*, (Basel, Switzerland:Springer International Publishing, 2015), 82.

6 Caroline Bradbury-Jones and Louise Isham, "The pandemic paradox: The consequences of COVID-19 on domestic violence," *J Clin Nurs* 29, no. 13–14 (April 2020): 2047–49. https://doi.org/10.1111/jocn.15296.

7 Jacob Kagi, "Crime Rate in WA Plunges Amid Coronavirus Social Distancing Lockdown Measures," *ABC News Australia*, April 7, 2020, https://www.abc .net.au/news/2020-04-08/coronavirus-shutdown-sees-crime-rate- drop-in-wa/12132410.

8 Shelly M. Wagers, "Domestic Violence Growing in Wake of Coronavirus Outbreak," *The Conversation*, April 8, 2020, https://theconversation.com/ domestic-violence-growing-in-wake-of-coronavirus-outbreak-135598.

9 "Climate Change," Church World Service, accessed September 10, 2021, https://cwsglobal.org/learn/climate-change/?gclid=CjwKCAjwoZWH-BhBgEiwAiMN66e43FGYojuYWKtR9w2v4AR3go9TkmhtyiGjb-vIaAM-RKZkLrQV4XxBoCmSEQAvD_BwE.

10 "Social Impact Storytelling," Georgetown University School of Continuing Study, The Economist Executive Education Navigator, accessed September 10, 2021, https://execed.economist.com/georgetown-school -continuing-studies/social-impact-storytelling-2021-10-01.

11 James M. Kouzes and Barry Posner, *Encouraging the Heart: A Leader's Guide to Rewarding and Recognizing Others*, (New Dehli, India: Wiley India Pvt. Ltd., 2008), Kindle.

12 David L. Cooperrider, Diana Kaplan Whitney, and Jacqueline M. Stavros, *Appreciative Inquiry Handbook: The First in a Series of AI Workbooks for Leaders of Change* (Etobicoke, ON, Canada: Lakeshore Communications, 2003), 3.

13 "The 4-D Cycle," BJ Seminars International, accessed September 10, 2021, https://bjseminars.com.au/our-approach/appreciative-inquiry/ the-4-d-cycle/.

14 Pascal Wallisch, "Two Years Later We Finally Know Why People Saw 'The Dress' Differently," *Slate*, April 12, 2017, https://slate.com/technology/2017/04/heres-why-people-saw-the-dress-differently.html.

15 "How to Harmonize Heart and Brain Gregg Braden," video, August 1, 2018, 12:32, https://www.youtube.com/watch?v=GG_aTtjUcCw.

16 Sarah Pruitt, "7 Things You Might Not Know About the Women's Suffrage Movement," *History*, updated February 26, 2021, https://www.history.com/news/7-things-you-might-not-know-about-the-womens-suffrage-movement.

17 "Address to Joint Session Of Congress May 25, 1961," John F. Kennedy Presidential Library and Museum, National Archives, accessed September 11, 2021, https://www.jfklibrary.org/learn/about-jfk/historic-speeches/ address-to-joint-session-of-congress-may-25-1961.

18 "Rafael Nadal Biography," The Famous People, accessed August 23, 2021, https://www.thefamouspeople.com/profiles/rafael-nadal-6053. php.

19 "Women Leaders in Education: Mastering Authenticity, Influence and Power Through Embodied Leadership," Teachers College Columbia University, May 14–15, 2020, https://www.tc.columbia.edu/continuing -professional-studies/programs/all-offerings/developing-embodied -leadership/.

20 Mehrad Nazari, interviewed by the authors, September 8, 2020.

21 Howard J. Curzer, *Aristotle's Painful Path to Virtue.* Journal of the History of Philosophy 40 (2):141–162 (2002).

22 Brené Brown, *Dare to Lead: Brave Work. Tough Conversations. Whole Hearts.*, (New York: Penguin Random House L.L.C., 2018), 186.

23 "National Culture," Hofstede Insights, accessed September 10, 2021, https://hi.hofstede-insights.com/national-culture.

24 Amrit Dhillon, "Selective Abortion in India Could Lead to 6.8m Fewer Girls Being Born by 2030," *The Guardian,* August 21, 2020, https://www. theguardian.com/global-development/2020/aug/21/selective-abortion- in-india-could-lead-to-68m-fewer-girls-being-born-by-2030.

25 Ruhi Kandhari, "Girls Interrupted," *Down To Earth,* April 25, 2011, https://www.downtoearth.org.in/blog/girls-interrupted-33385.

26 Olivier, "India's Missing Daughters—Desire to Have a Male Child and Female Infanticide in India," Humanium, March 15, 2018, https:// www.humanium.org/en/indias-missing-daughters-desire-male-child -female-infanticide-india/.

27 https://www.thehansindia.com/andhra-pradesh/gender-ratio-declines -due-to-foeticides-in-kadapa-distrct-590833, accessed 11/10/2021

28 Don Miguel Ruiz, *The Four Agreements: A Practical Guide to Personal Freedom,* Amber-Allen Publishing, July 10, 2018.

29 "About Us," African Library Project, accessed September 10, 2021, www.AfricanLibraryProject.org/about-us/.

30 "SHE-CAN," SHE-CAN, accessed September 10, 2021, www.shecan. global/.

31 "We Care Solar," WeCareSolar.org, accessed September 10, 2021, wecaresolar.org/.

32 "National Bonner Leaders Program," Virginia Wesleyan University,

accessed September 10, 2021. https://www.vwu.edu/campus-life/wesleyan-engaged/national-bonner-leaders.php/pdfs/2012-and-2016-NSLVE-Report-Virginia-Wesleyan-College.pdf.

33 Fred Luskin, *Forgive for Good: A Proven Prescription for Health and Happiness* (New York: HarperCollins Publishers, 2003), x.

34 "Cleveland Clinic: Mission, Vision & Values," Cleveland Clinic, accessed October 23, 2021, https://my.clevelandclinic.org/about/overview/who-we-are/mission-vision-values.

35 "DukeHealth: Mission, Vision & Values," Duke University Health System, accessed October 23, 2021, https://corporate.dukehealth.org/who-we-are/mission-vision.

36 "Kaiser Permanente: Who We Are," Kaiser Permanente, accessed October 23, 2021, https://about.kaiserpermanente.org/who-we-are.

37 "Bon Secours: Mission," Bon Secours Health System, accessed October 23, 2021, https://www.bonsecours.com/about-us/mission#:~:text-t=News%20Contact%20Us-,Our%20Mission,are%20poor%2C%20dying%20and%20underserved.

38 United Nations Department of Economic and Social Affairs, "Women's Job Market Participation Stagnating at Less than 50% for the Past 25 Years, Finds UN Report," *United Nations*, accessed October 29, 2021, https://www.un.org/en/desa/women's-job-market-participation-stagnating-less-50-past-25-years-finds-un-report.

39 Tam O'Neil and Pilar Domingo, "Women and Power: Overcoming Barriers to Leadership and Influence," GSDRC Applied Knowledge Services, accessed October 29, 2021, https://gsdrc.org/document-library/women-and-power-overcoming-barriers-to-leadership-and-influence/.

40 Included with permission from Barbara Bylenga, Executive Director of SHE-CAN.

41 "Open a Door Foundation," Idealist, accessed November 6, 2021, https://www.idealist.org/en/nonprofit/2465eb70aa7c40e4a4a4069dafd d818f-open-a-door-foundation-san-rafael.

42 Amanda Ellis, "'Building Forward Better' – Why Women's Leadership Matters," International Leadership Association, August 12, 2020, https://

ilaglobalnetwork.org/building-forward-better-why-womens-leader-ship-matters/.

43 John Gerzema and Michael D'Antonio, *The Athena Doctrine: How Women (and the Men Who Think Like them) Will Rule the Future* (San Francisco: Jossey-Bass, 2013).

44 Tom Kelley with Jonathan Littman. "The 10 Faces of Innovation," *Fast Company,* October 1, 2005, https://www.fastcompany.com/54102/10-faces-innovation.

45 "Give Girls an Alternative," Amref Health Africa, accessed September 10, 2021, https://donate.amrefusa.org/campaign/give-girls-an-alternative/c178039.

46 Pat Obuchowski, "How to Get the Impact You Want," Thrive Global, September 8, 2020, https://thriveglobal.com/stories/how-to-get-the-impact-you-want/.

47 "Mark Twain: Quotes: Quotable Quote," Goodreads.com, accessed September 10, 2021, https://www.goodreads.com/quotes/2528-keep-away-from-people-who-try-to-belittle-your-ambitions.

48 "Roy T. Bennett: Quotes: Quotable Quote," Goodreads.com, accessed September 10, 2021, https://www.goodreads.com/quotes/7553679-listen-with-curiosity-speak-with-honesty-act-with-integrity-the, accessed 7/23/2021.

49 The World Bank, "Poverty Incidence in Kenya Declined Significantly, but Unlikely to be Eradicated by 2030," WorldBank.org, April 10, 2018, https://www.worldbank.org/en/country/kenya/publication/kenya-economic-update-poverty-incidence-in-kenya-declined-significantly-but-unlikely-to-be-eradicated-by-2030.

50 Haley Hine, "Girls Education in Kenya," The Borgen Project, May 10, 2018, https://borgenproject.org/girls-education-in-kenya/.

51 William Bridges and Susan Mitchell, "Leading Transition: A New Model for Change," Berlin, Eaton & Associates Ltd., accessed September 10, 2021, http://www.crowe-associates.co.uk/wp-content/uploads/2013/08/WilliamBridgesTransitionandChangeModel.pdf.

52 Autumn Spanne, "The Lucky Ones: Native American Tribe Receives $48M to Flee Climate Change," *The Guardian,* March 23, 2016, https://

www.theguardian.com/environment/2016/mar/23/native-ameri-can-tribes-first-nations-climate-change-environment-indican-remov-al-act.

53 "3Strands Global Foundation," 3Strands Global Foundation, accessed September 11, 2021, https://www.3strandsglobalfoundation.org/.

54 "Sex Trafficking Statistics," Guardian Group, accessed September 11, 2021, https://guardiangroup.org/sex-trafficking-statistics/?gclid=C-jwKCAjwj6SEBhAOEiwAvFRuKIcD4551en9b8_qeh4p5GpSUl-wIBI4lTHT5PglLVbjH77fA8hSMTyRoCWosQAvD_BwE.

55 The World Bank, "Gender-Based Violence (Violence Against Women and Girls)," WorldBank.org, September 25, 2019, https://www.worldbank.org/en/topic/socialsustainability/brief/violence-against-women-and-girls.

56 UN Women, "Facts and figures: Ending violence against women," UNWomen.org, updated March 2021, https://www.unwomen.org/en/what-we-do/ending-violence-against-women/facts-and-figures.

57 "Country Comparisons: Maternal Mortality Rate," CIA.gov: The World FactBook, accessed September 11, 2021, https://www.cia.gov/the-world-factbook/field/maternal-mortality-rate/country-comparison.

58 "Community Solutions," IREX, accessed September 11, 2021, https://www.irex.org/project/community-solutions.

59 "Promoting Gender Equality in the World of Work," International Labour Organization, accessed September 11, 2021, https://www.ilo.org/ankara/projects/gender-equality/lang--en/index.htm.

60 "Destiny Reflection," DestinyReflection.org, accessed September 11, 2021, https://destinyreflection.org/.

61 "The Mind Can Be a Dangerous Place or a Great Gift," Sounds True, accessed September 11, 2021, https://product.soundstrue.com/living-from-a-place-of-surrender/free-video-series/#a_aid=5dfbb27a 13fea&a_bid=05fc7a8f.

62 Guest Contributor, "Maasai Culture & History: Understanding the Soul of East Africa," Zegrahm Expeditions, January 29, 2018, https://www.zegrahm.com/blog/maasai-culture-history-understanding-soul-east-africa.

63 "Peter Block: Quotes," Goodreads, accessed September 11, 2021, https://www.goodreads.com/author/quotes/144322.Peter_Block.

64 Lifewater, "How Many Countries Don't Have Clean Water? Top 10 List and Facts," Lifewater blog, June 4, 2020, https://lifewater.org/blog/how-many-countries-dont-have-clean-water-top-10-list-and-facts/?gclid=CjwKCAjw9uKIBhA8EiwAYPUS3LIn42sF3EGkkqysMER_fksPl-xLp13zNn2si_TCVfMri0e6fXcO3BoCx1EQAvD_BwE.

65 Bethany Caruso, "To Empower Women, Give Them Better Access to Water," Emory News Center, March 22, 2016, https://news.emory.edu/stories/2016/03/er_caurso_conversation/campus.html.

66 James M. Kouzes and Barry Posner, *Encouraging the Heart: A Leader's Guide to Rewarding and Recognizing Others*, (New Dehli, India: Wiley India Pvt. Ltd., 2008), Kindle.

67 "AbilityPath: Inspiring Inclusion," AbilityPath.org, accessed September 11, 2021, https://abilitypath.org/.

68 Mehrad Nazari, interviewed by the authors, September 8, 2020.

69 Emily Esfahani Smith, "On Coronavirus Lockdown? Look for Meaning, Not Happiness," the *New York Times,* April 7, 2020, https://www.nytimes.com/2020/04/07/opinion/coronavirus-mental-health.html.

70 Caroline Castrillon, "Why Women Don't Need More Seats at the Table," *Forbes,* January 18, 2019, https://www.forbes.com/sites/carolinecastrillon/2019/01/18/why-women-dont-need-more-seats-at-the-table/?sh=94bc-3da1ac3e.

71 Jenifer Kuadli, "Women Entrepreneur Statistics," Legaljobs blog, February 2, 2021, https://legaljobs.io/blog/women-entrepreneurs-statistics/.

72 Anita Borg, interviewed by the authors, May 17, 2001.

73 Otto Scharmer and Katrin Kaufer, *Leading from the Emerging Future: From Ego-System to Eco-System Economies* (San Francisco: Berrett Koehler, 2013), 22.

About the Authors

Linda Alepin is a retired female executive and has served in leadership roles in large corporations, startups, consulting enterprises, academia, and the international nonprofit sector. She spent her early career breaking through the glass ceiling in the business world, went on to teach at the university level, and then pursued social justice globally through leadership education.

Linda's accomplishments include heading the team for a $2 billion corporate turnaround, raising $5 million for an early Internet startup that released its first product in eighteen months, consulting to high-tech companies about leadership, founding a global not-for-profit, creating a unique international experience for undergraduates, and rejuvenating a local social impact organization.

She has been featured in *Maslow on Management, and Gutsy Women Win,* and has written a chapter for *Leading Organizational Learning: Harnessing the Power of Knowledge.* She was the cover story of *Business Strategy Magazine* "Life Beyond the Mainframe" in 1995. Linda is a graduate of Stanford University and several state-of-the-art leadership curricula. She has spoken at numerous national conferences about leadership. Linda's vision is a world alive with love, peace, and justice. She believes that every person has the innate capability to be a leader in family, community, and the world.

Barbara E. Key is a teacher, consultant, and coach in Canada and the United States. She is passionate about facilitating leaders to achieve their vision for social change. She wants to shine her light so that others experience and express their own freedom. Coaching programs that she has designed and led have laid the foundation for the success of hundreds of social change projects benefitting thousands of community members.

Barbara coauthored You as a Global Leader (YAGL), a series of transformational leadership programs that educate people around the world to be more innovative, entrepreneurial, and team oriented. Even before the global pandemic, these curricula had been adapted for delivery asynchronously and synchronously over the Internet.

In 2017, twenty accomplished leaders attended Barbara's program. They have gone on to lead their organizations to new levels of accomplishment. The stories of six people from that course included in this book (Ashlie Bryant, Erin Montgomery, Philile Mkhize, Phionah Musumba, Florence Temu, and Priya Thakoor) illustrate their improved leadership competencies. Barbara's commitment is to a world in which each individual experiences freedom.

Notes